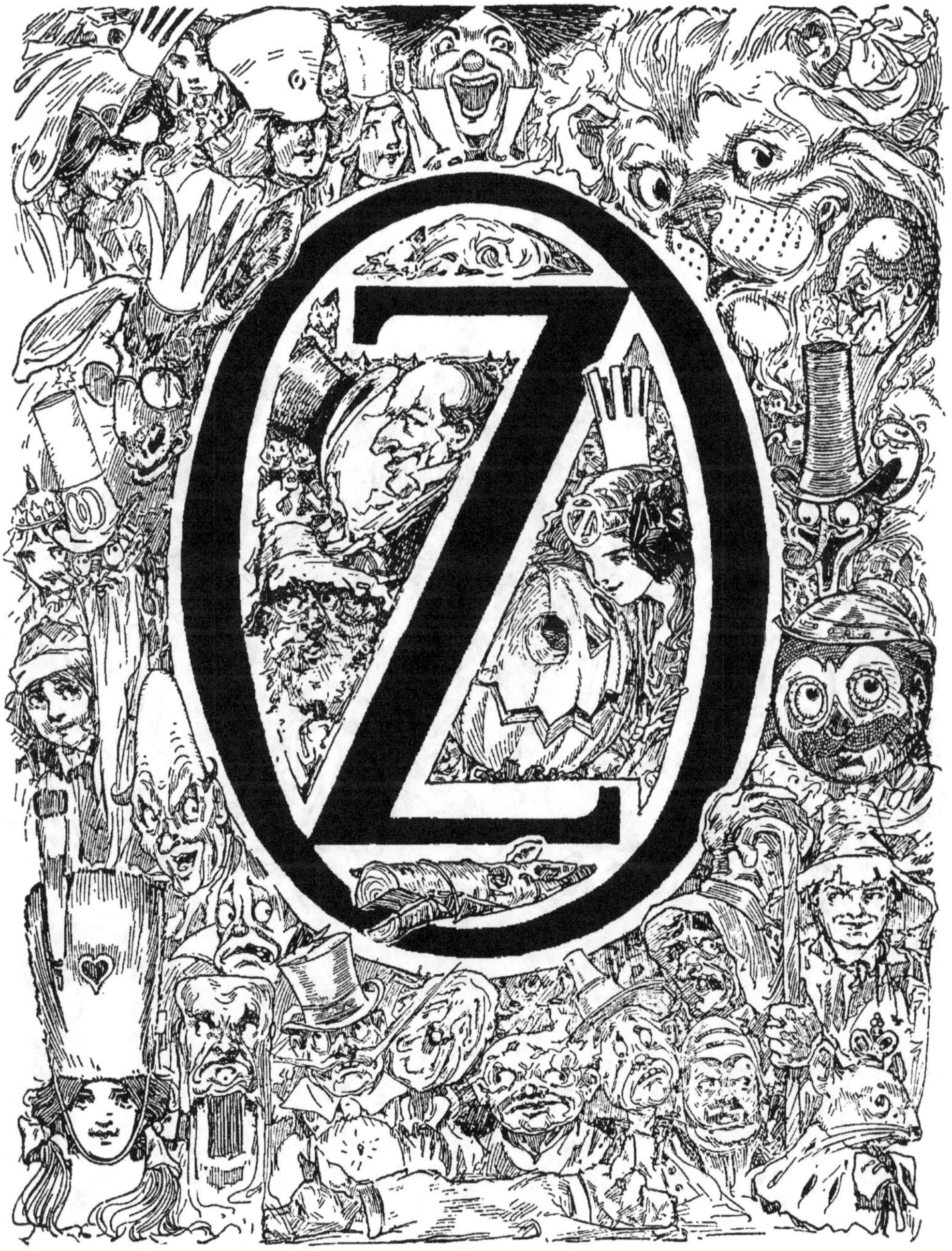

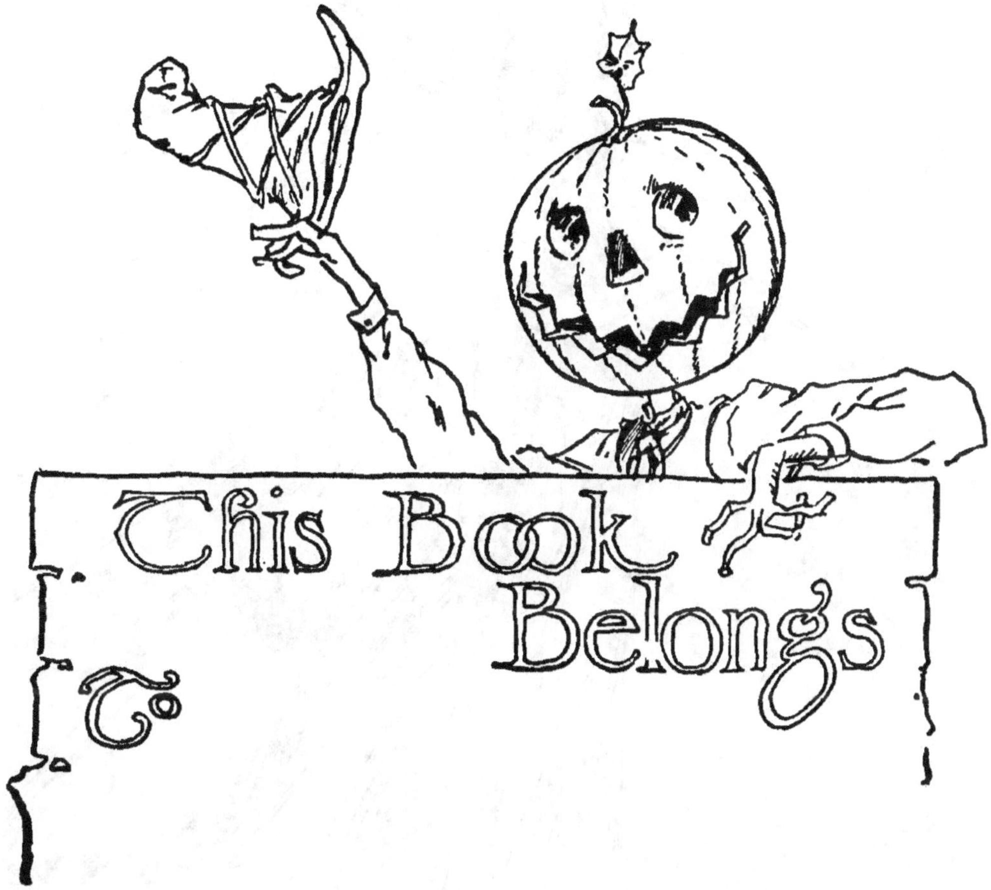
This Book
Belongs
To

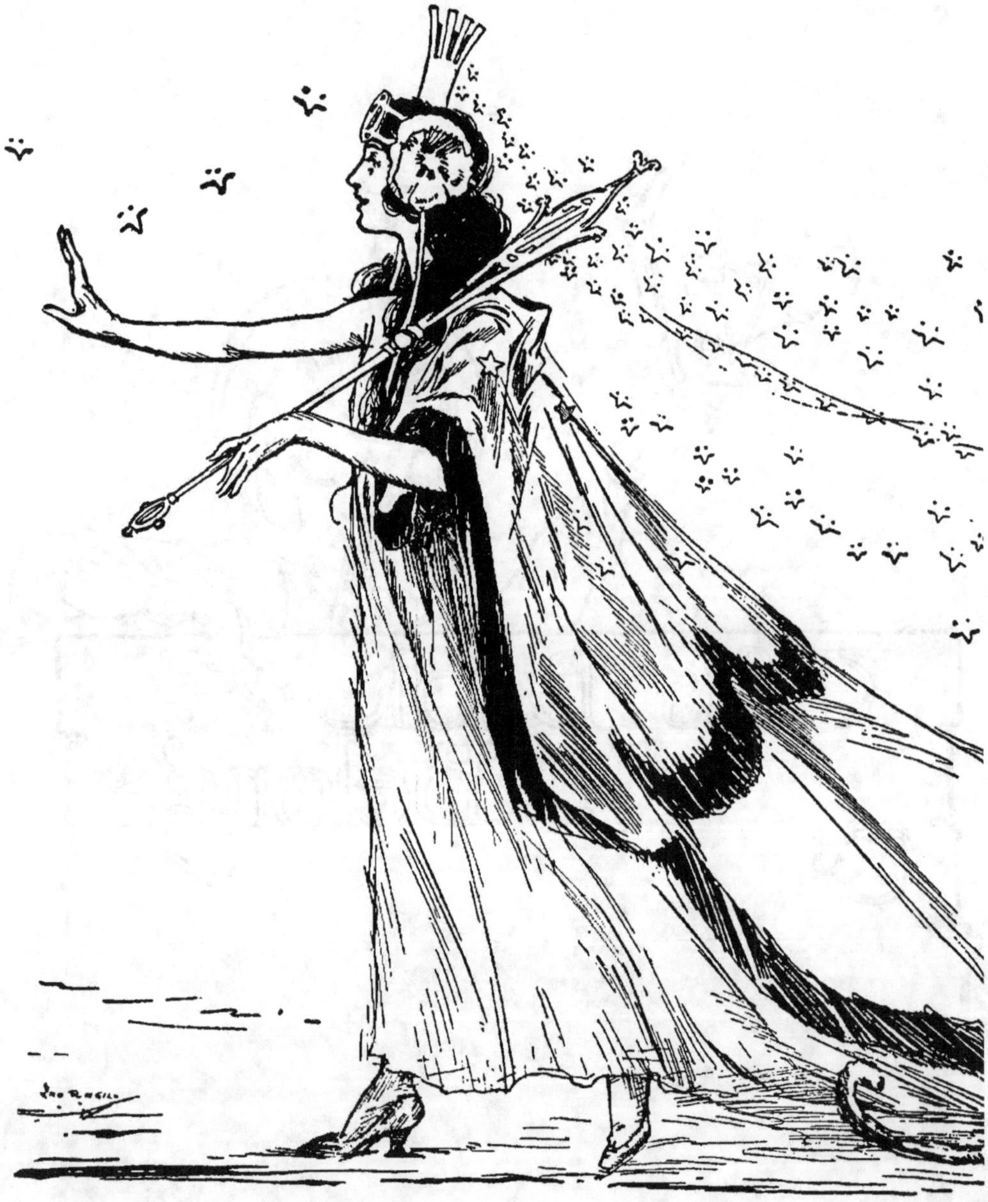

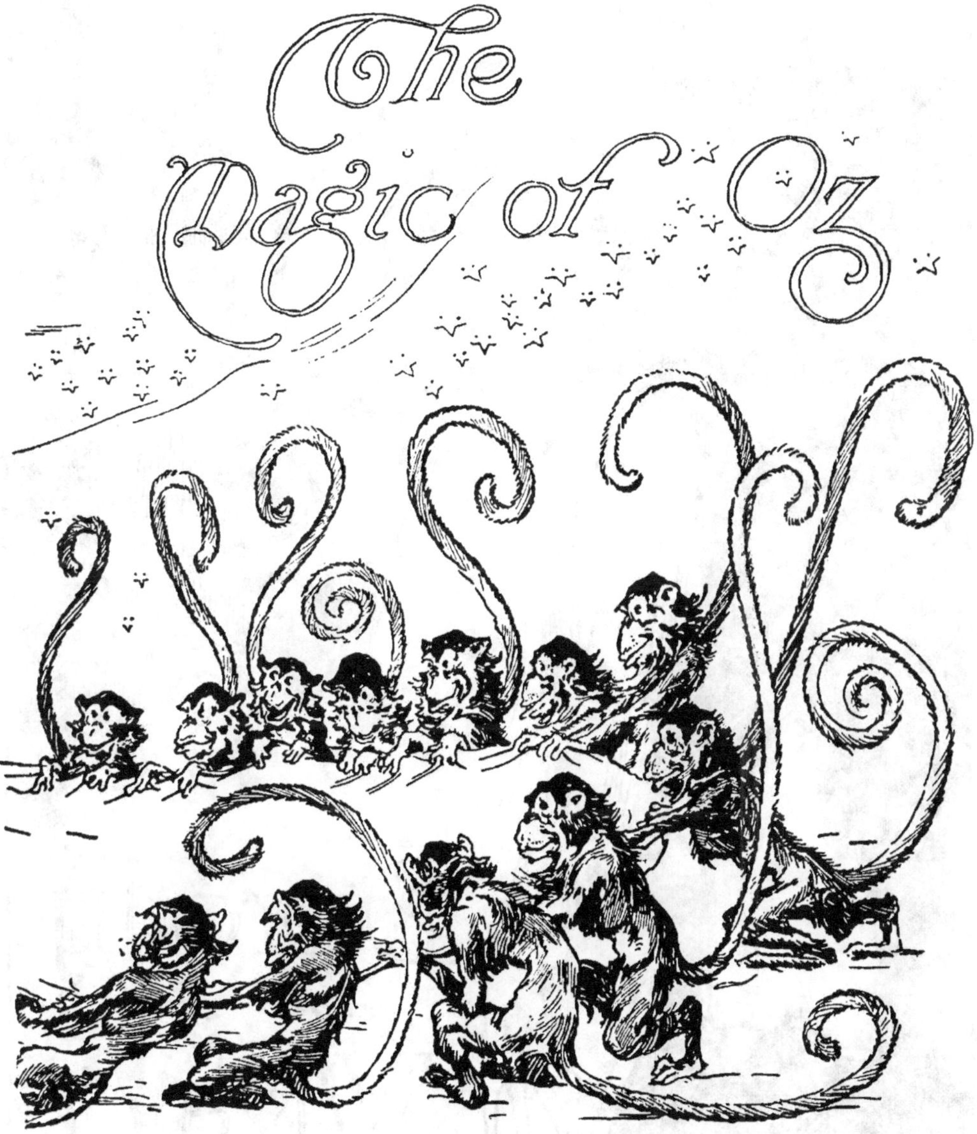
The Magic of Oz

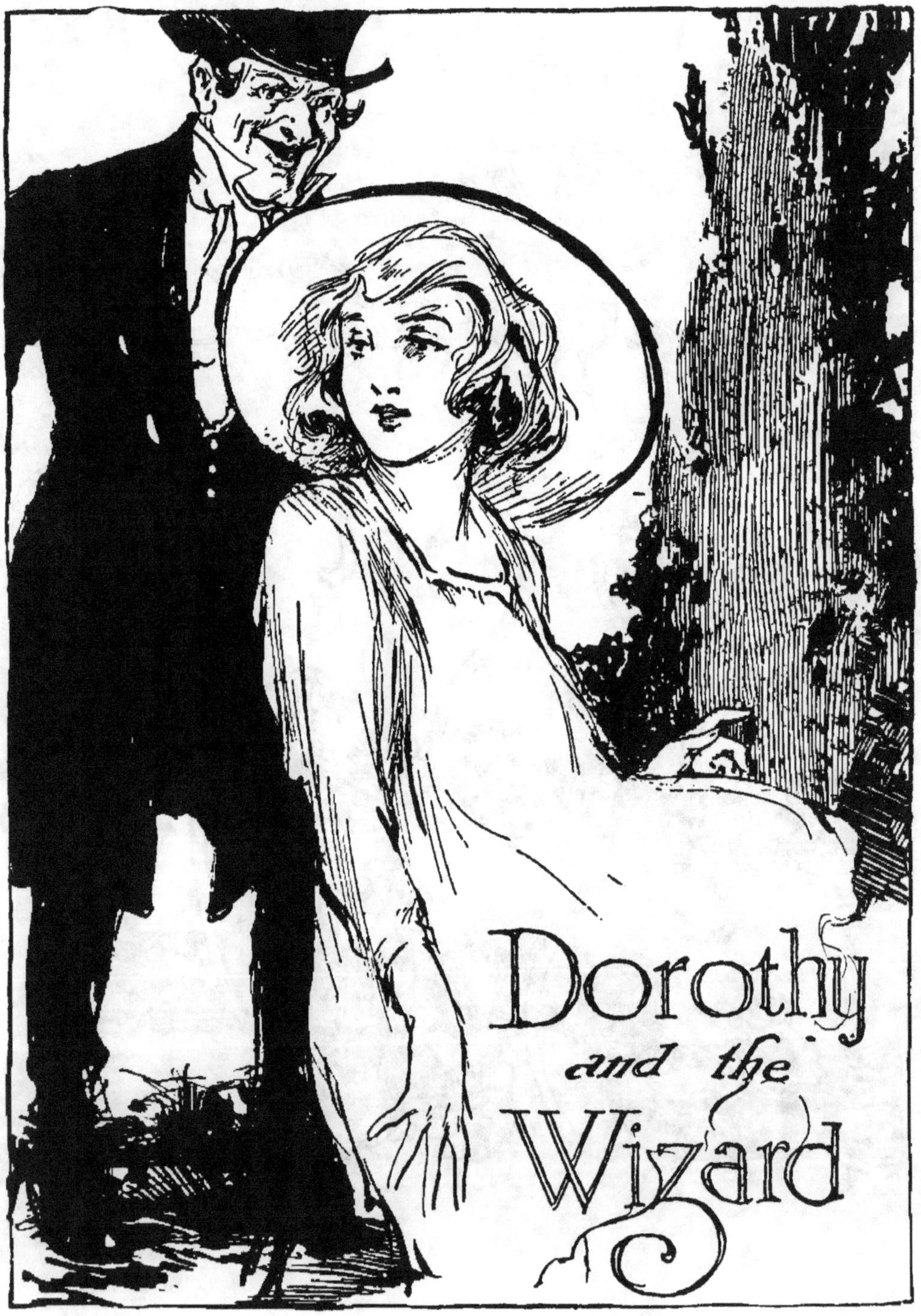
Dorothy
and the
Wizard

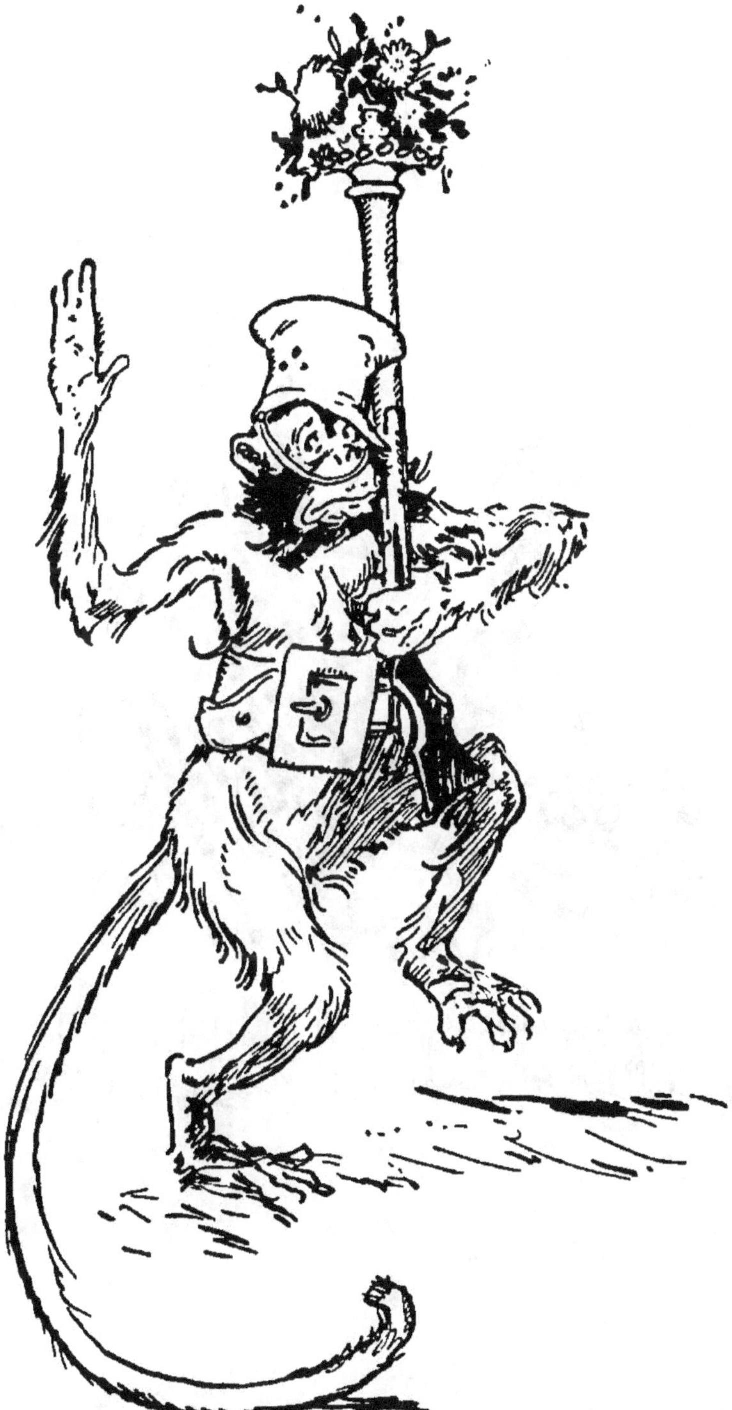

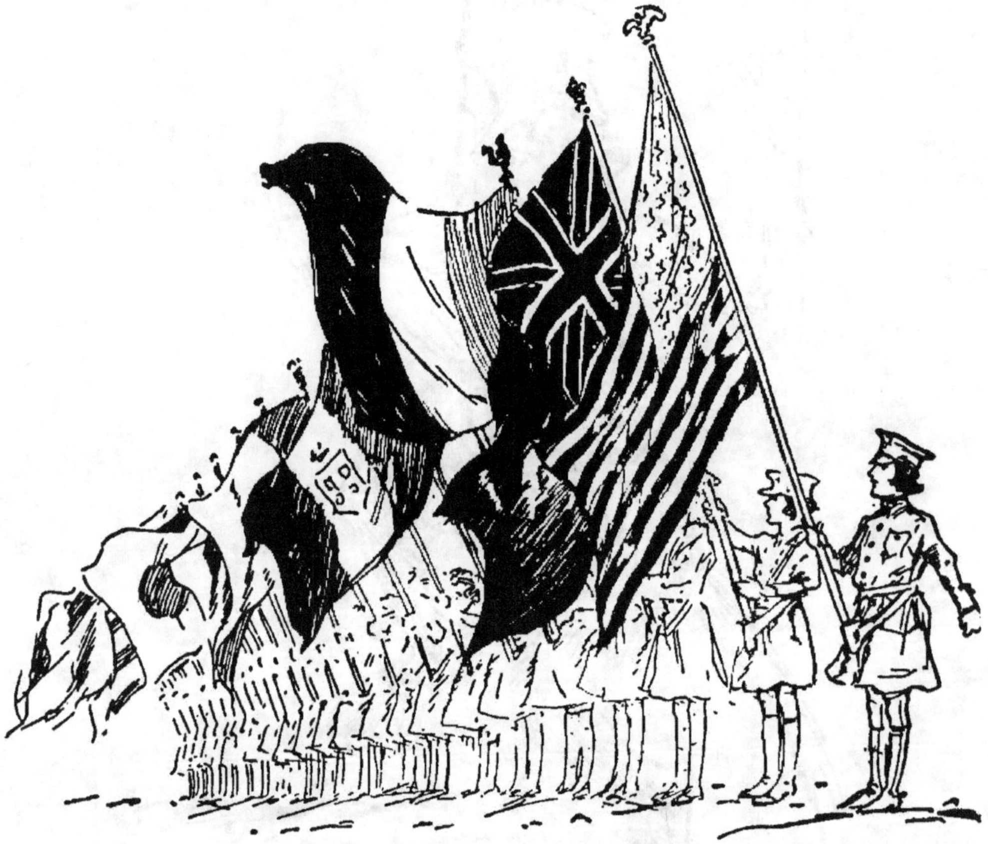

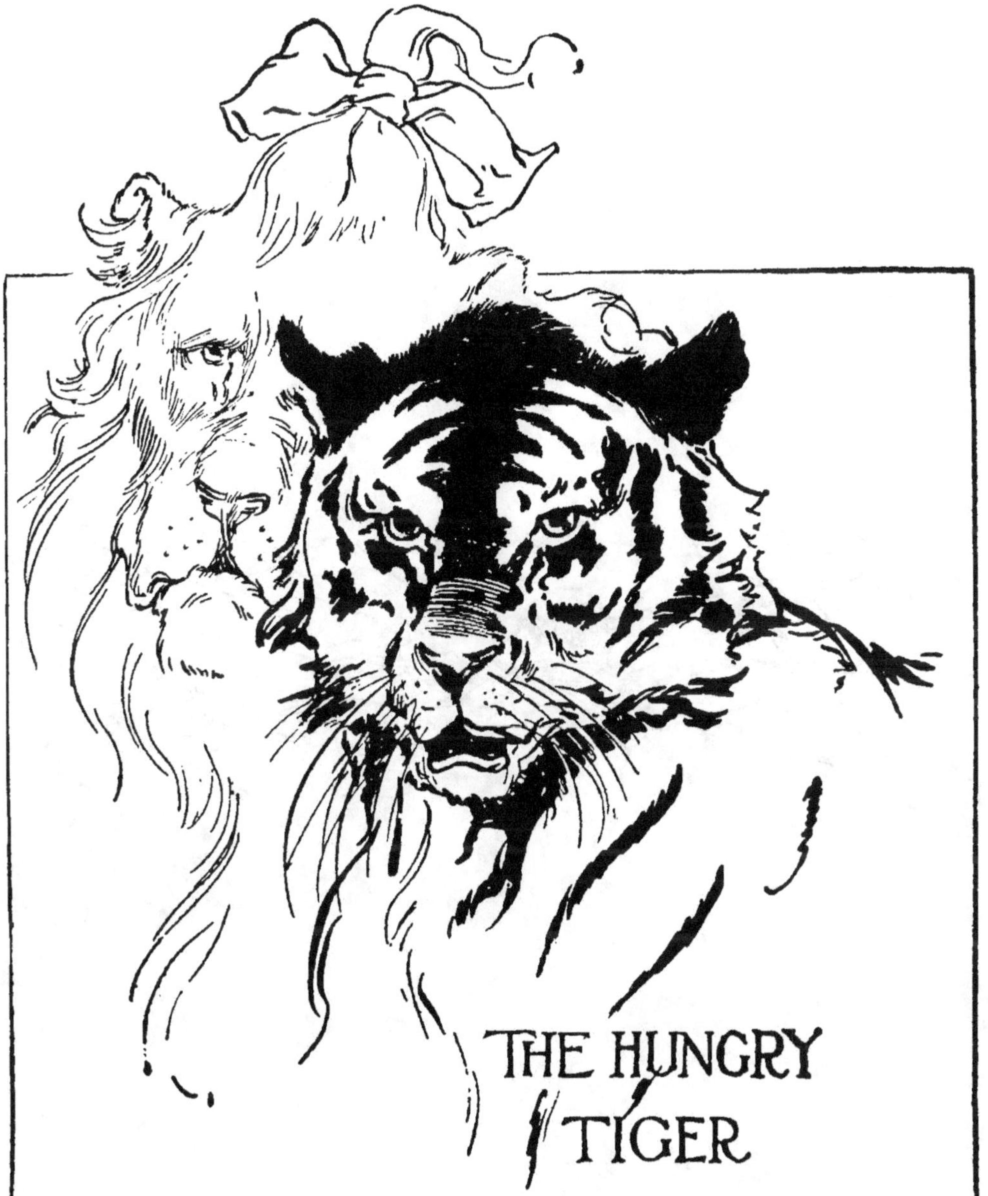
THE HUNGRY
TIGER
AND THE
COWARDLY LION

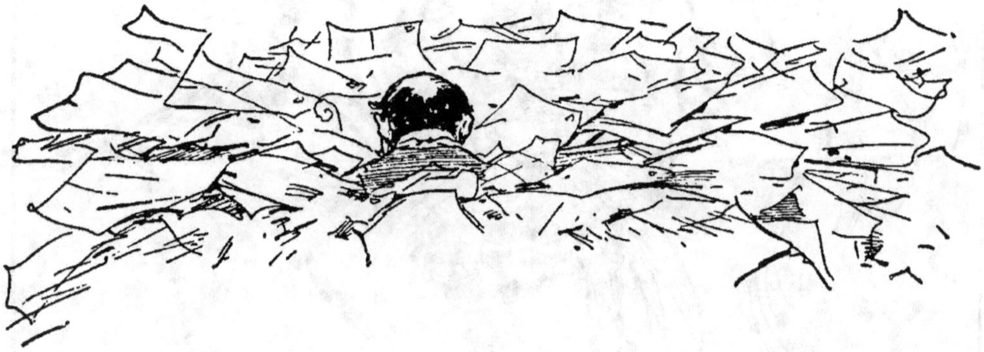

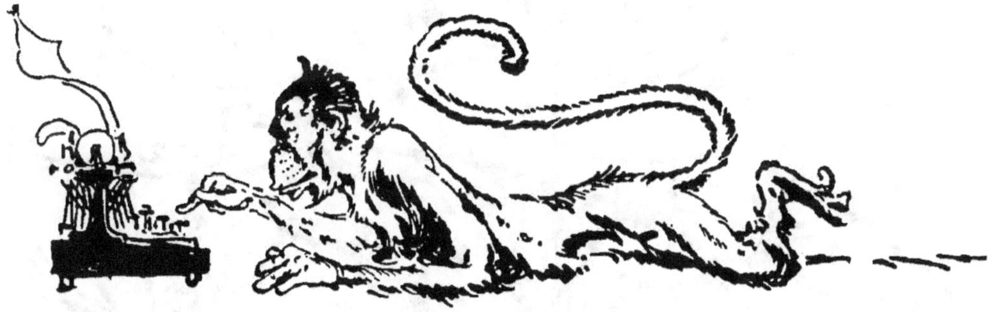

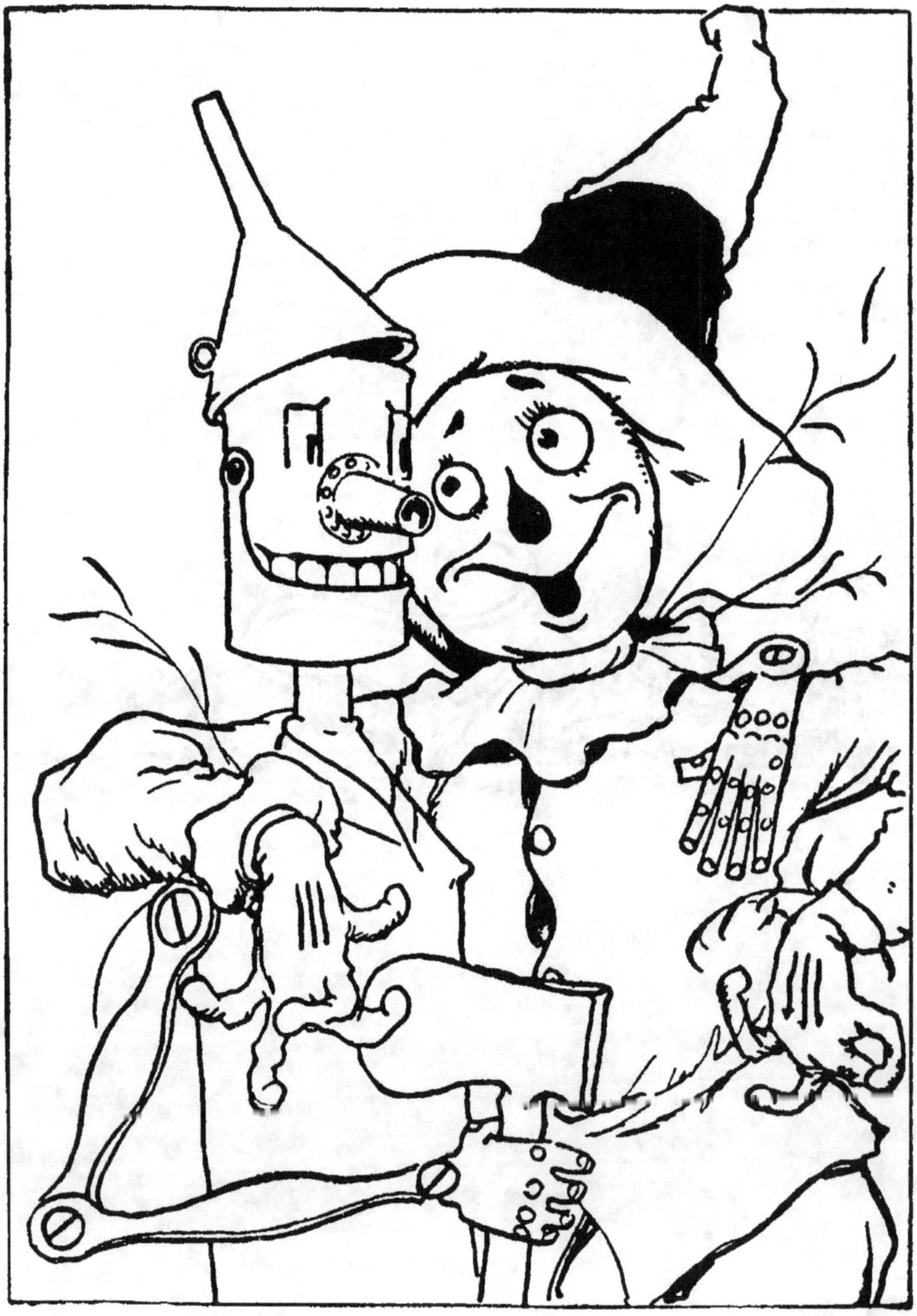

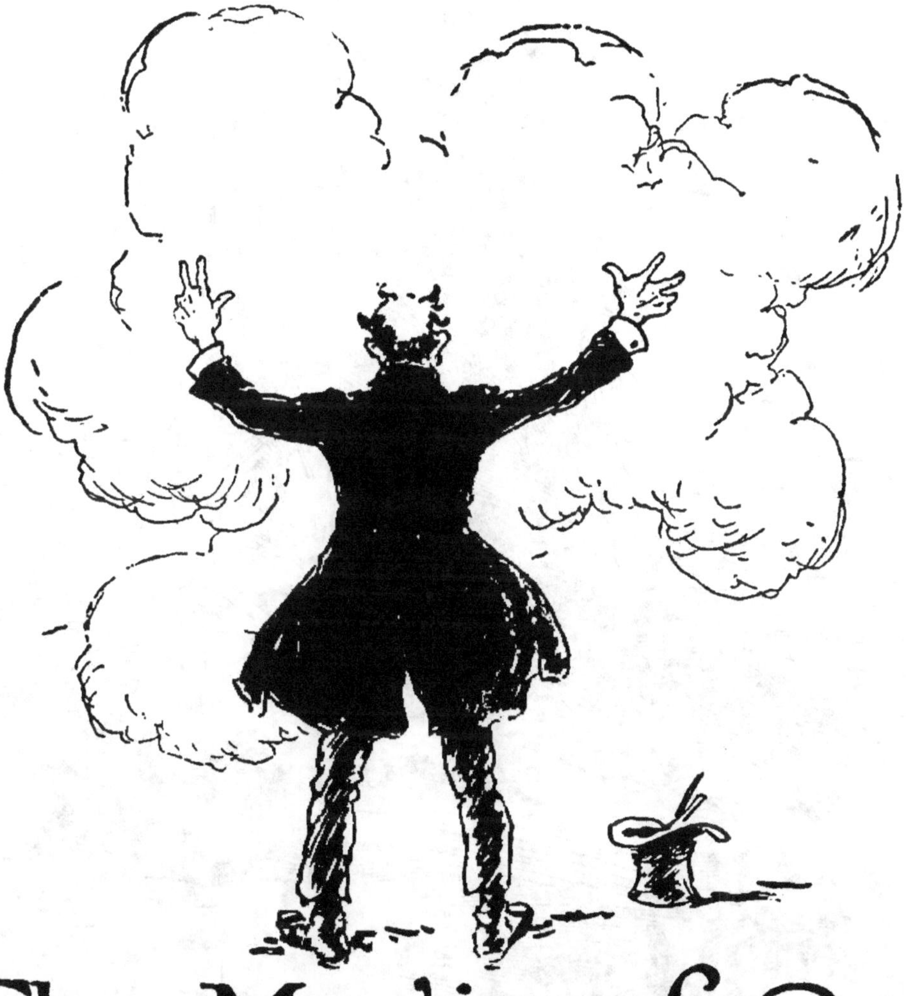

The Magic of Oz

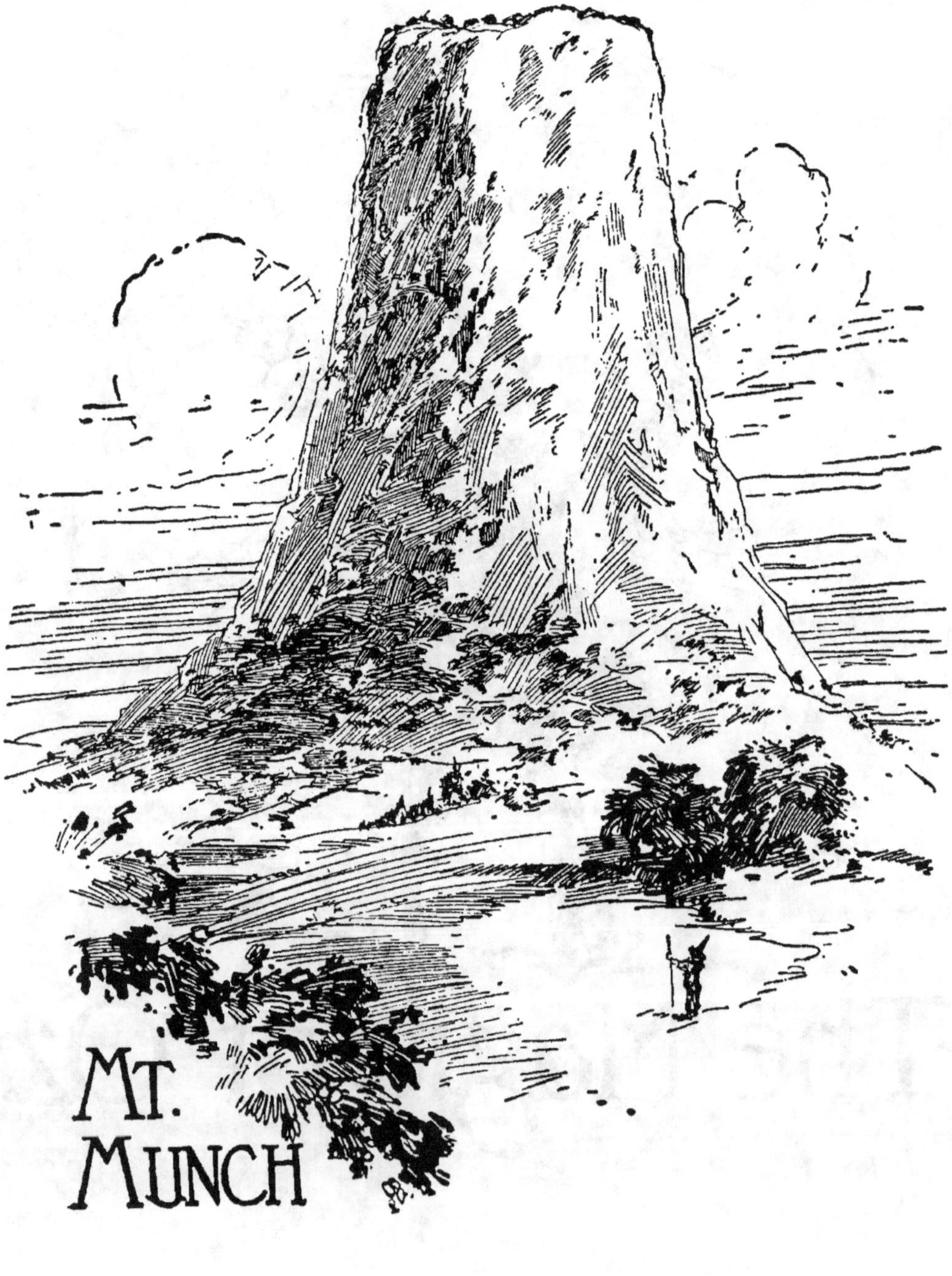
MT.
MUNCH

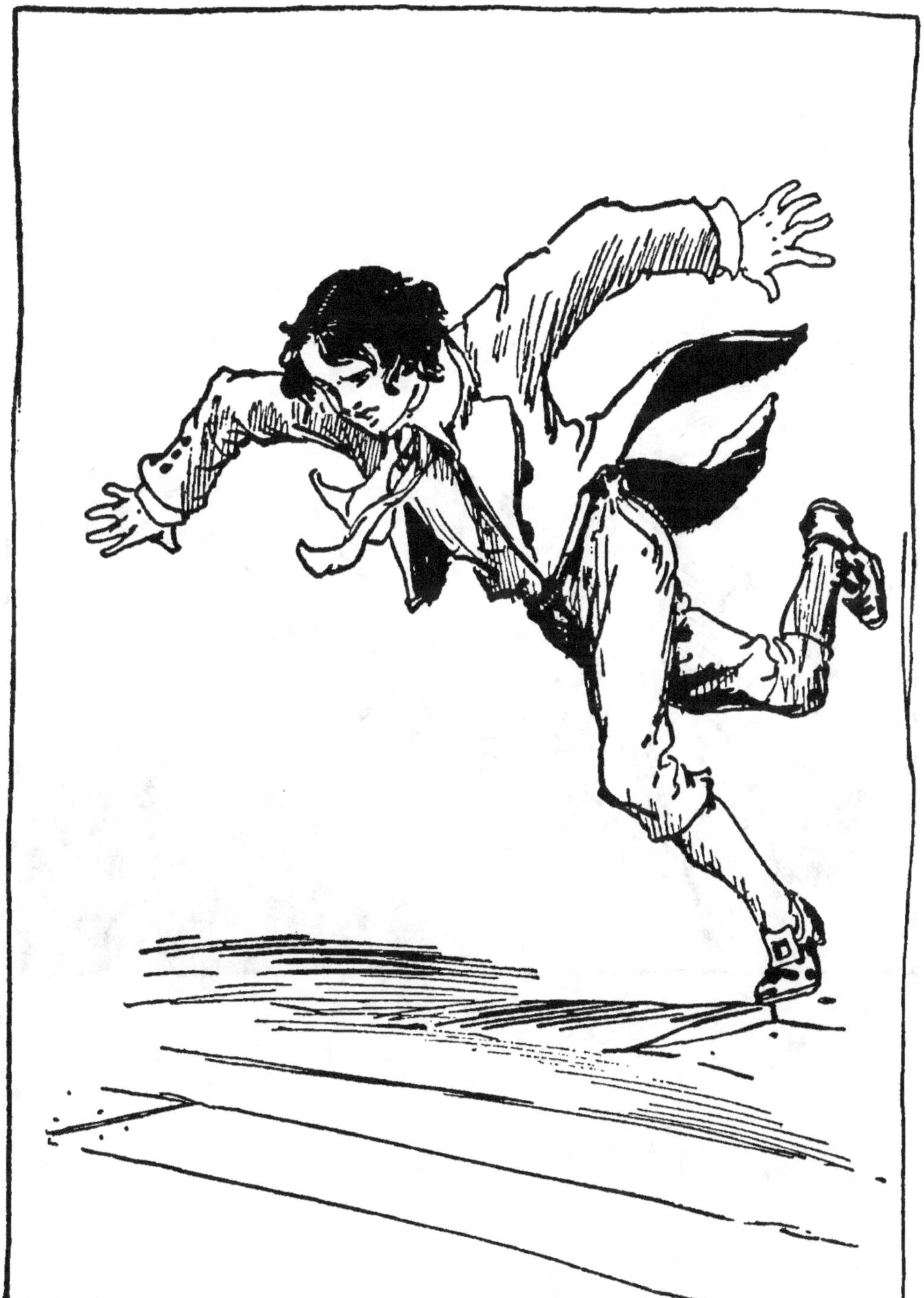

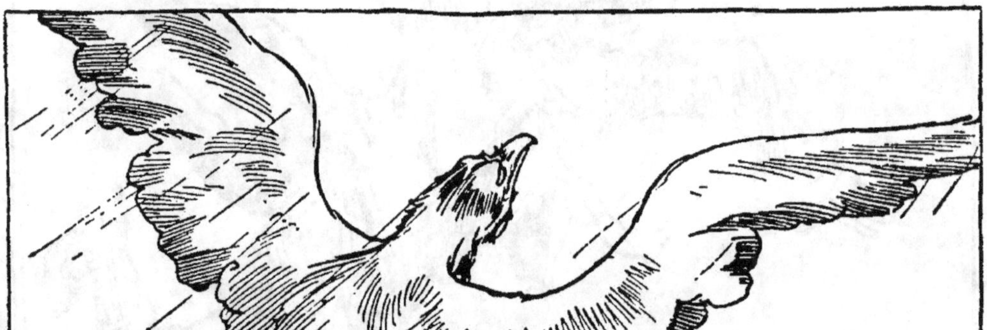

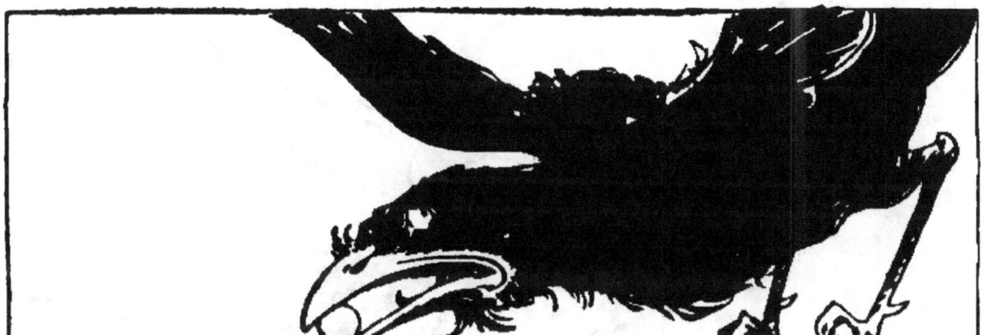

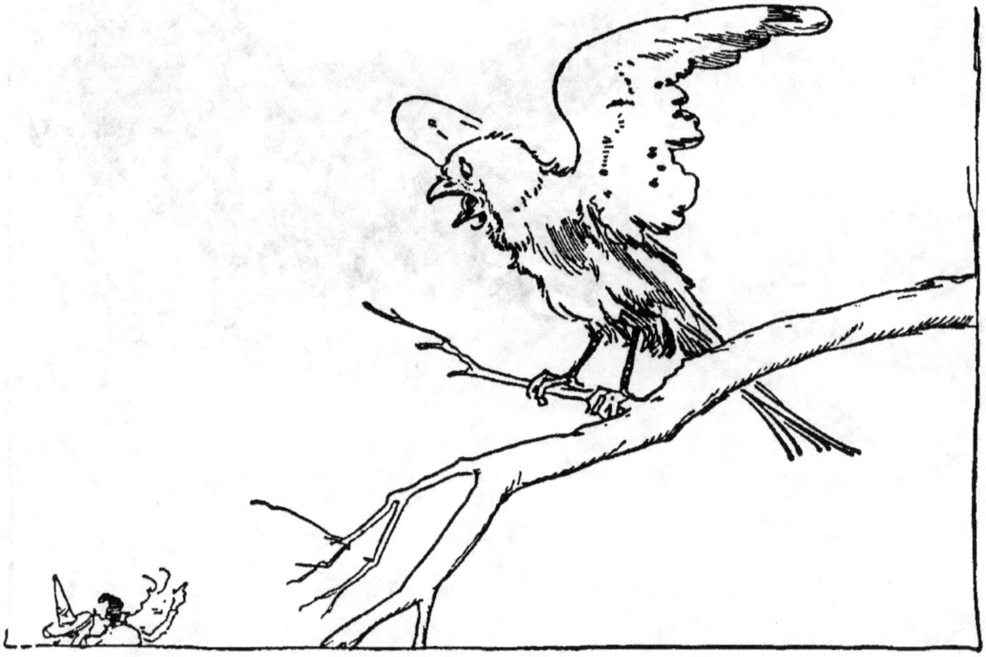

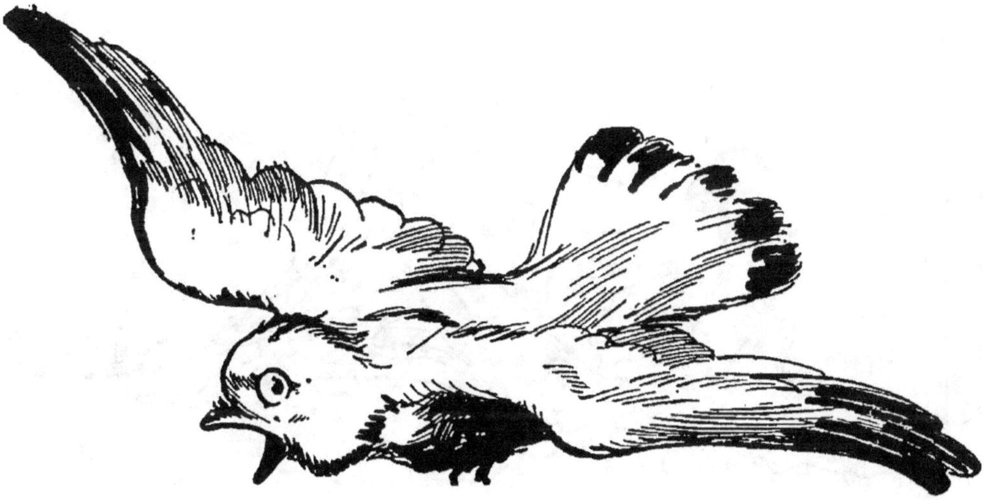

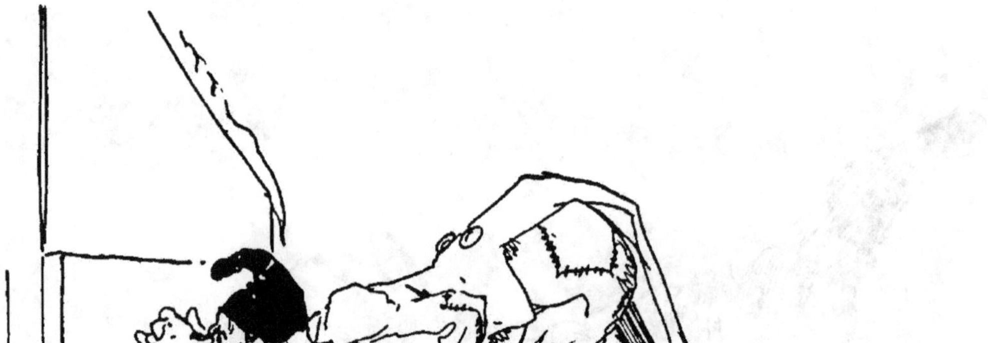

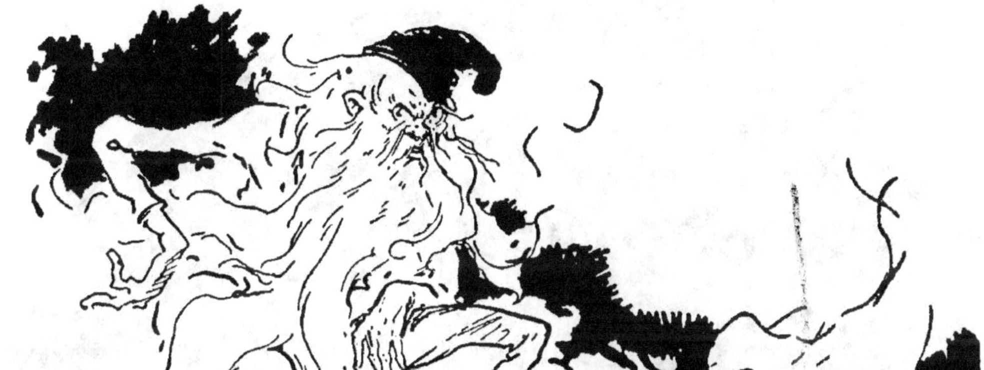

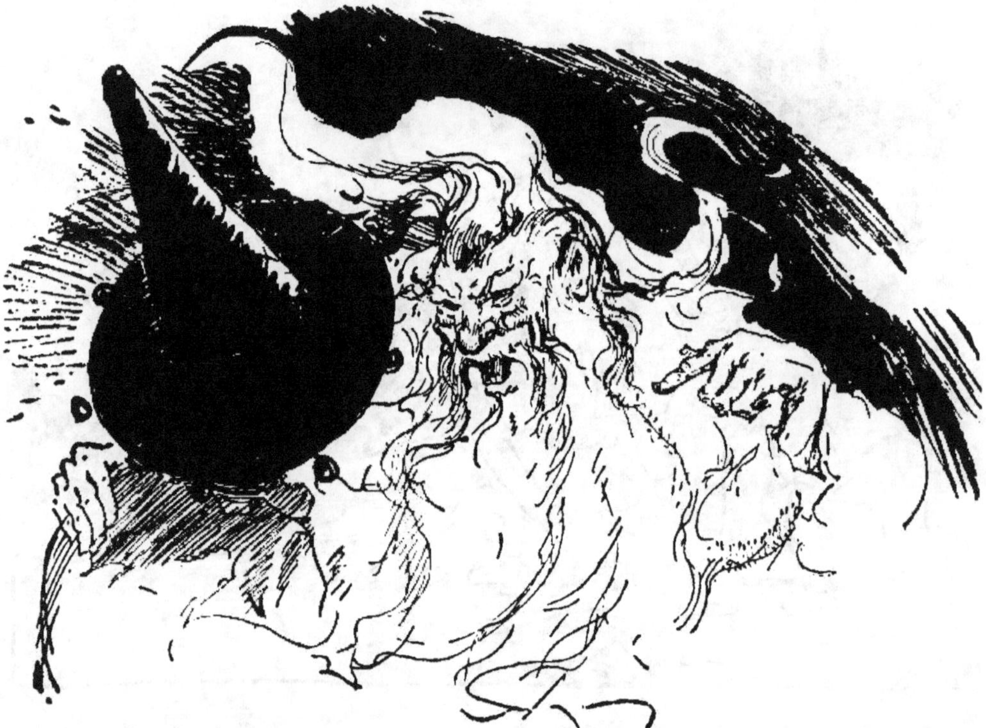

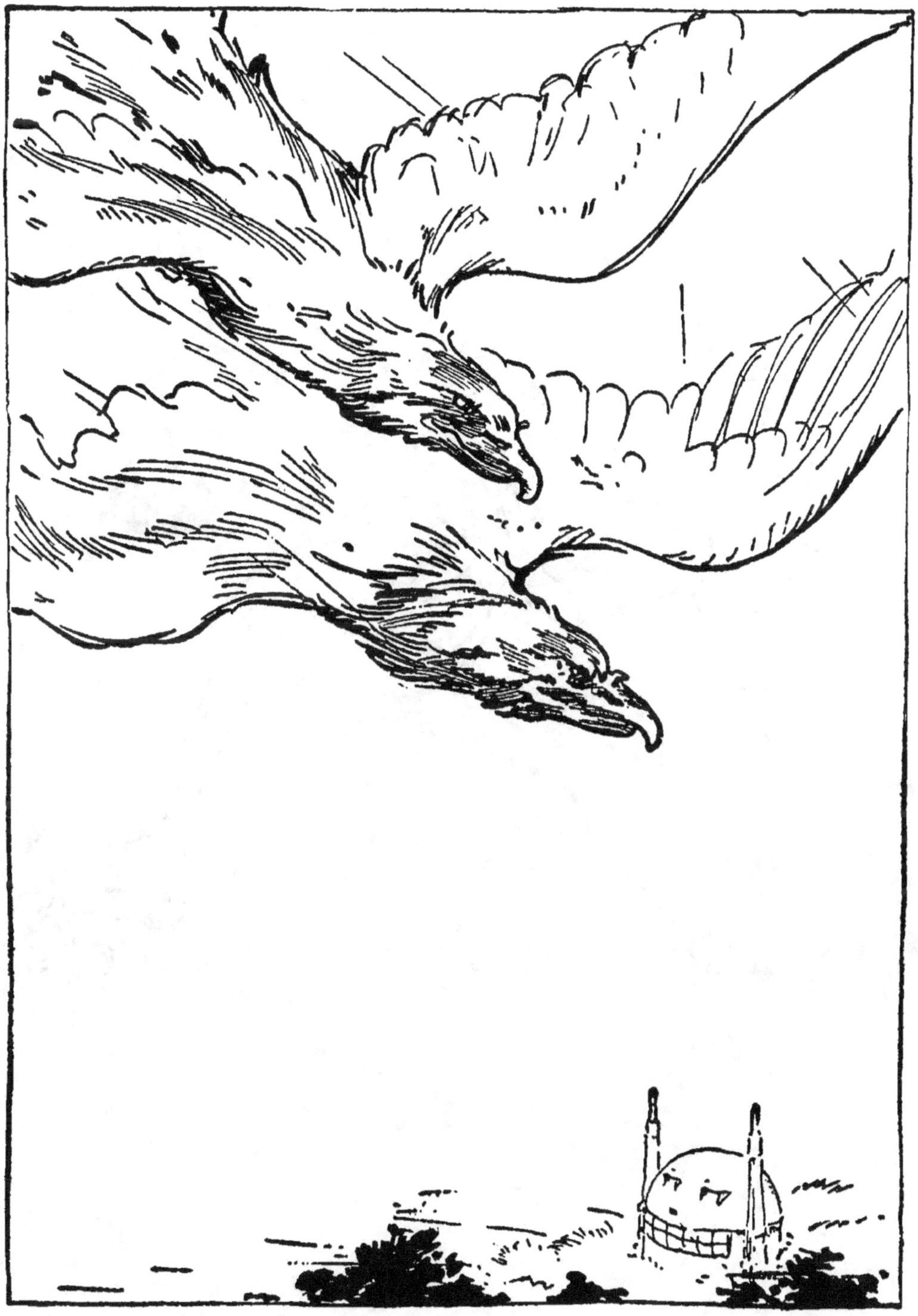

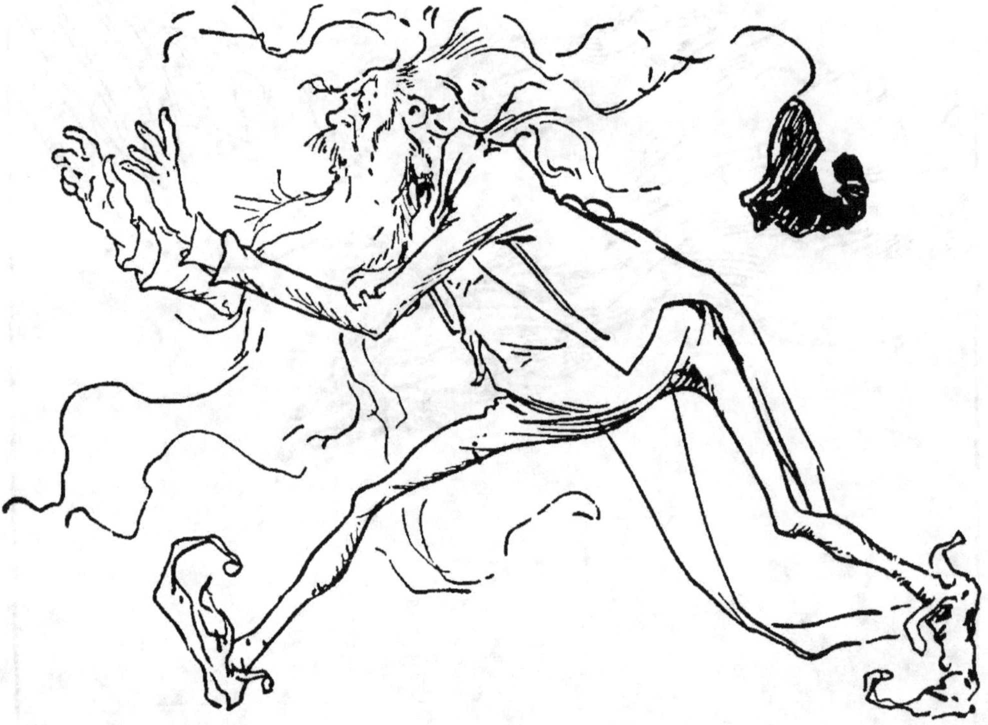

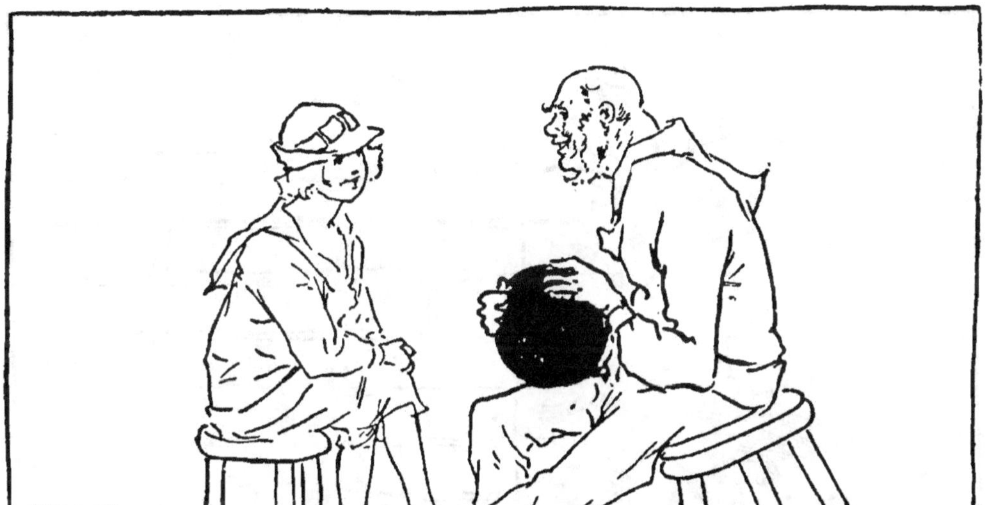

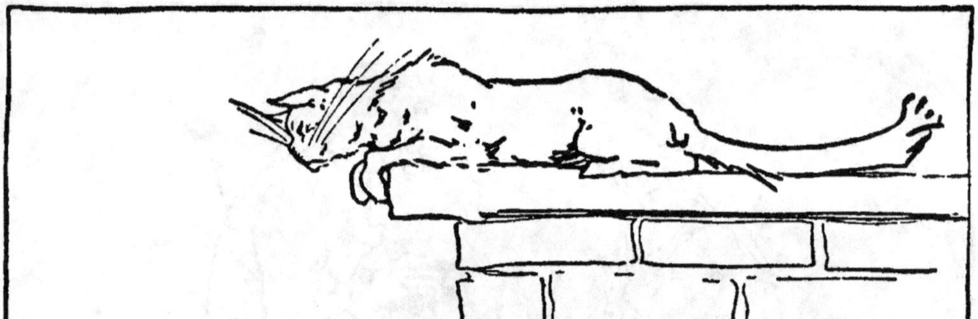

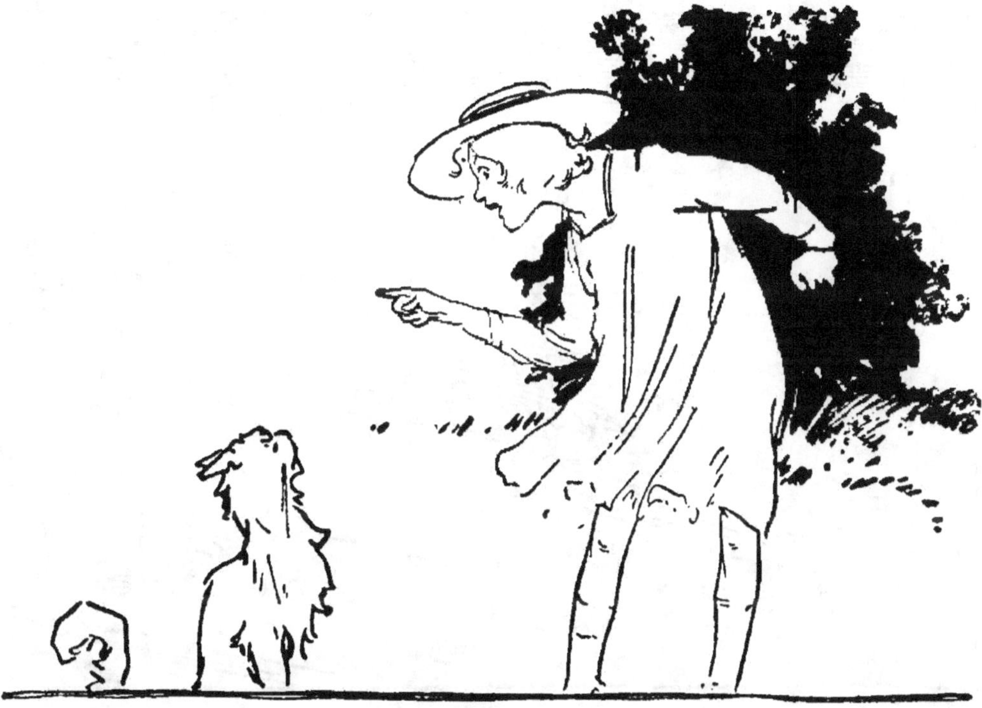

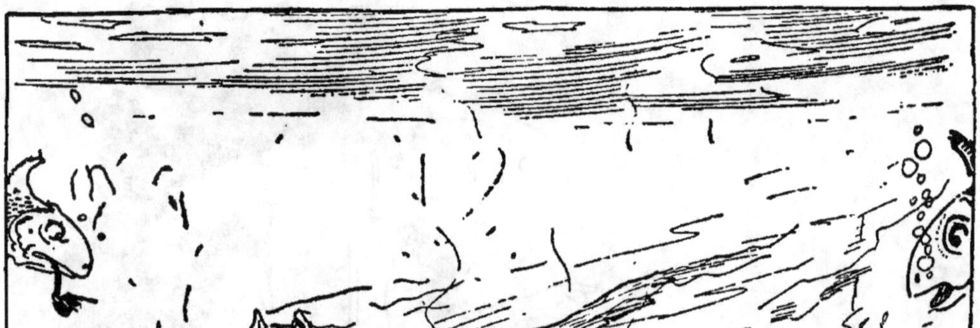

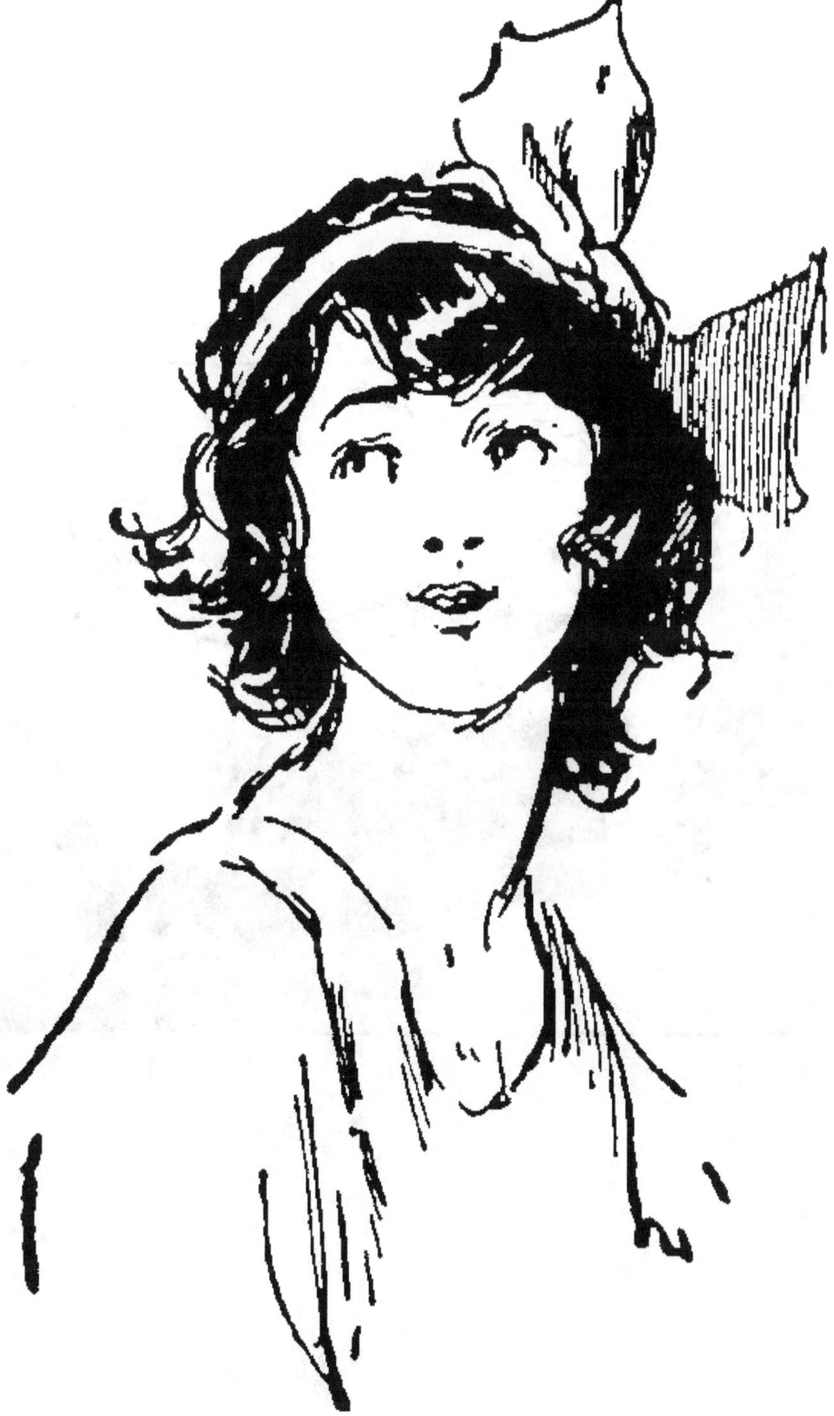

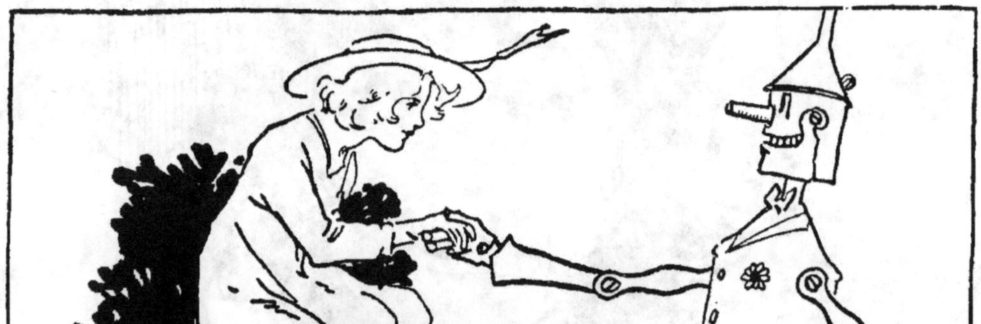

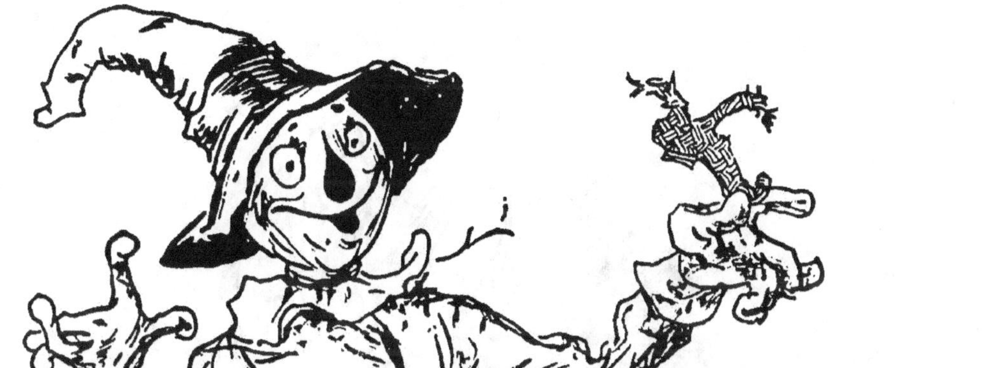

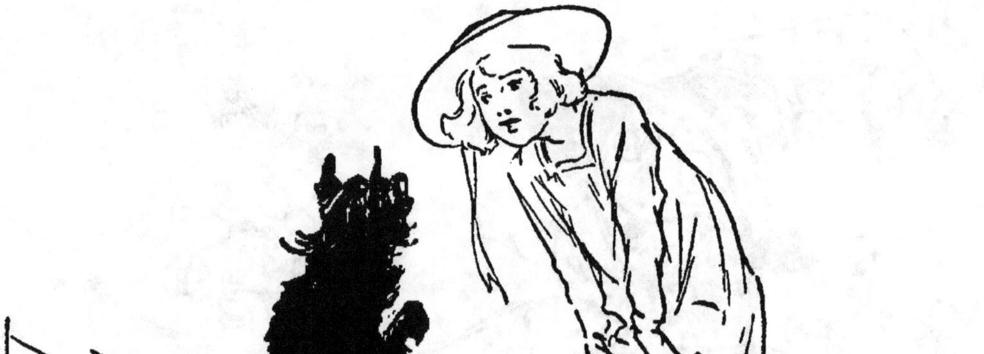

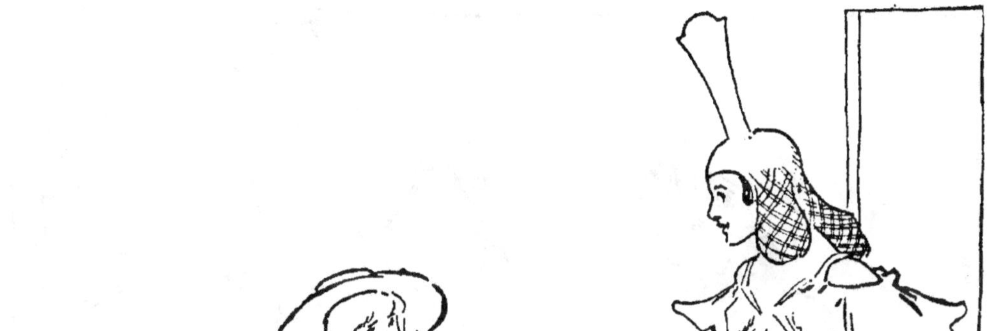

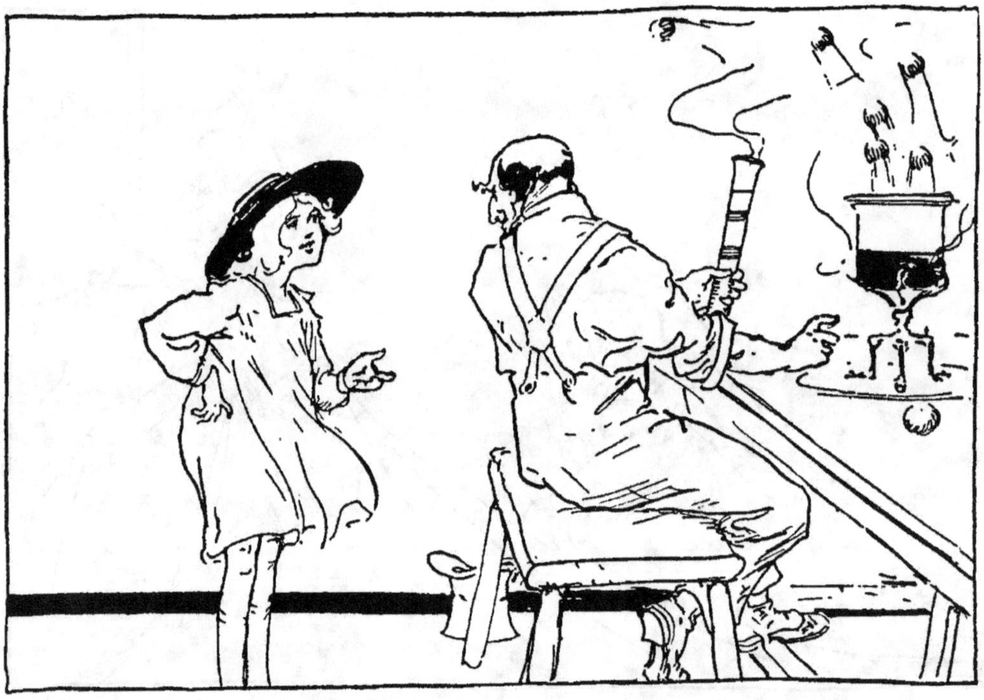

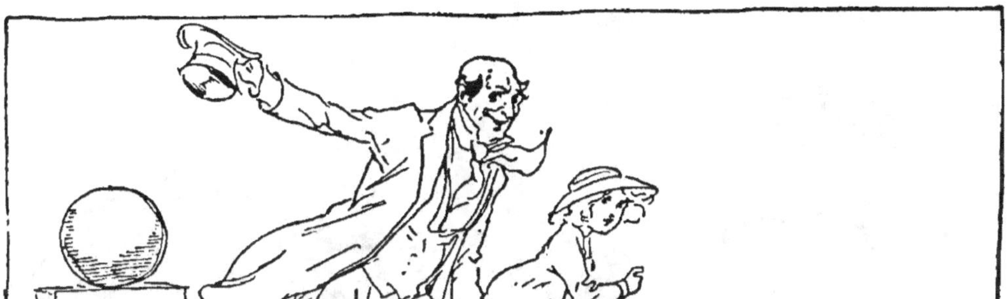

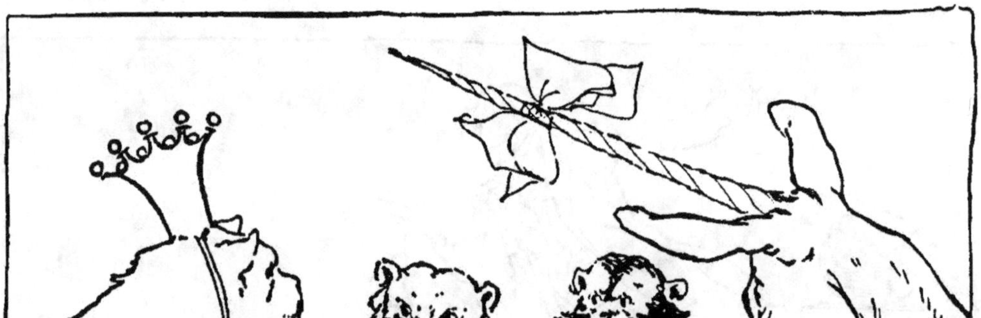

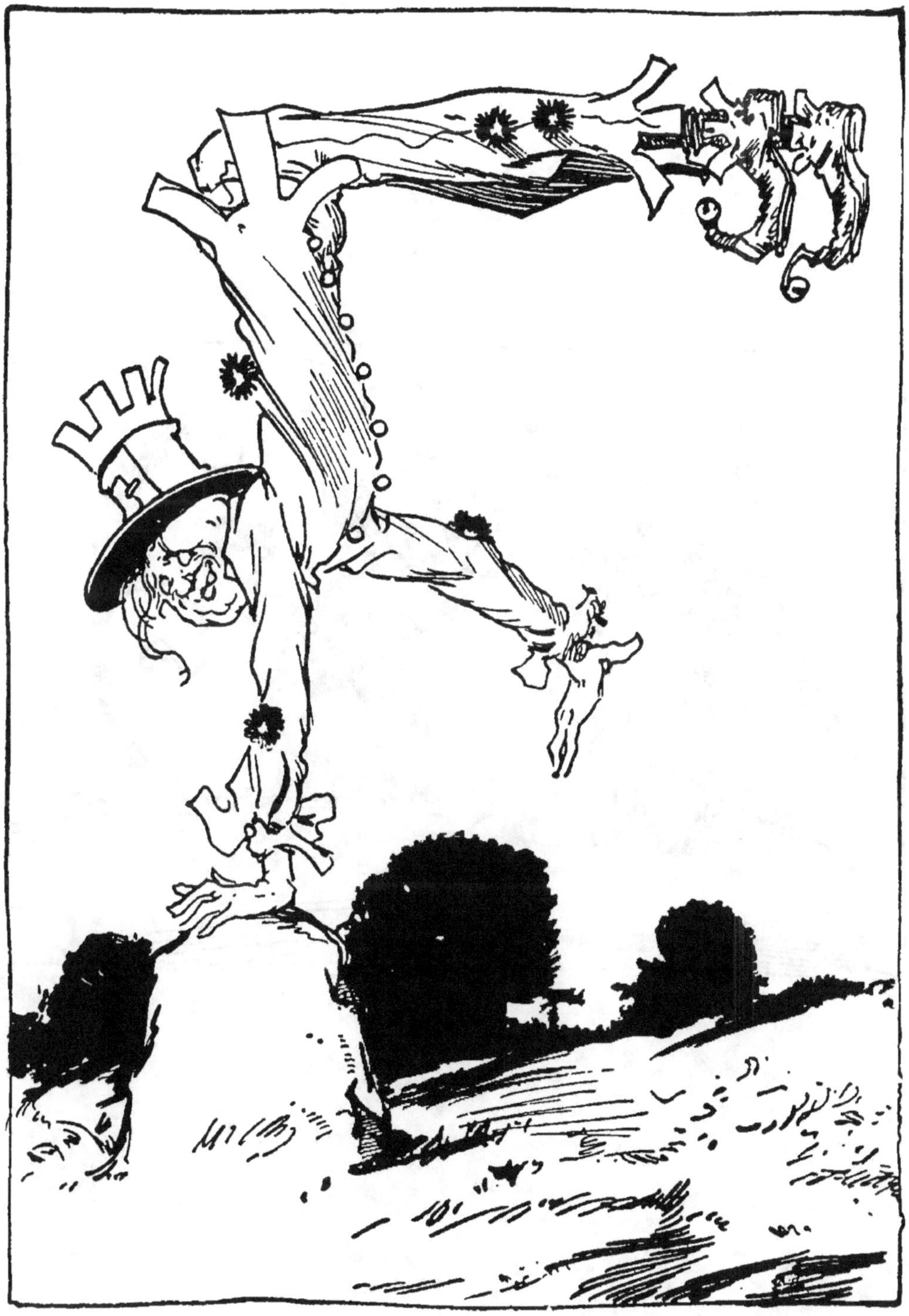

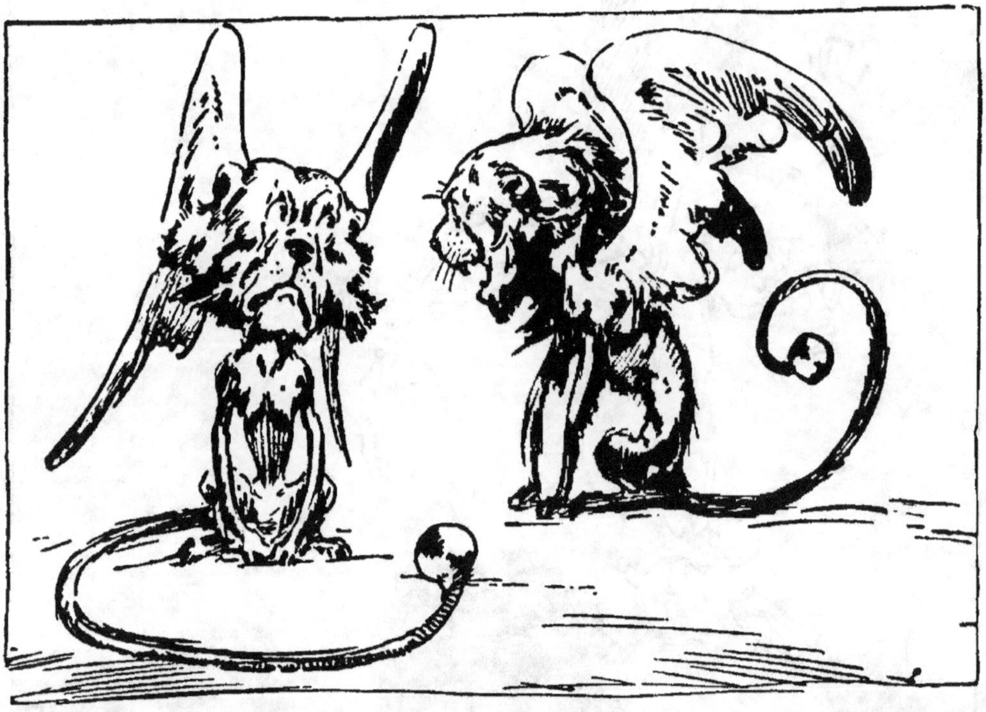

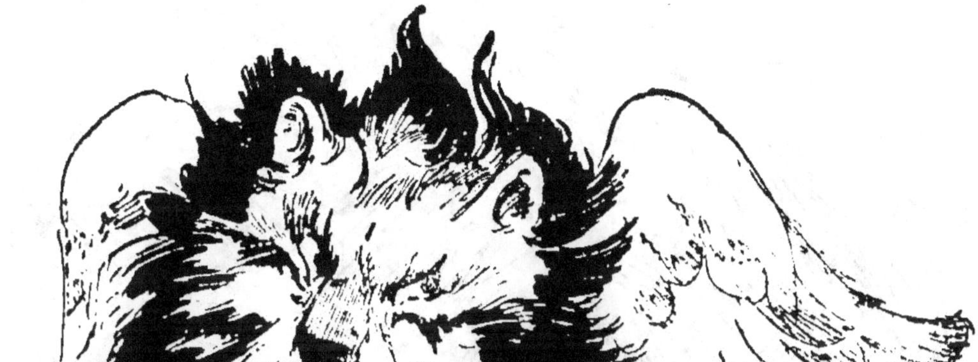

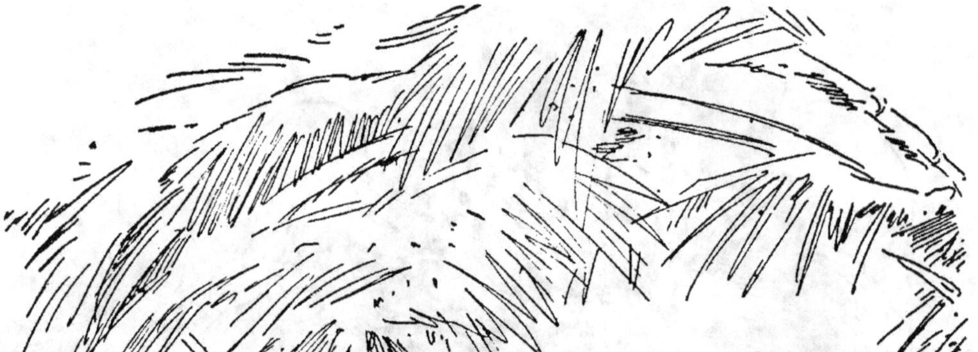

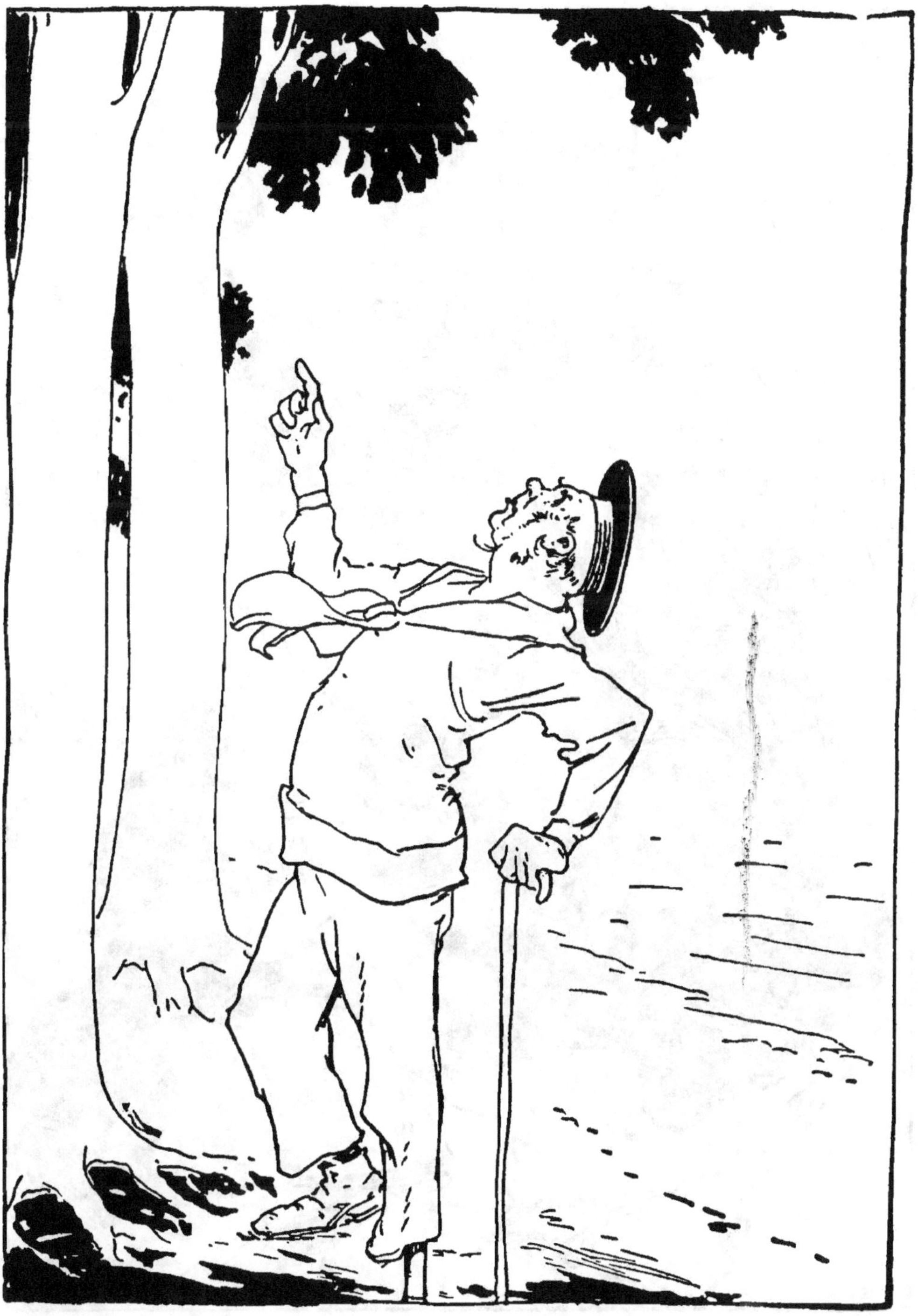

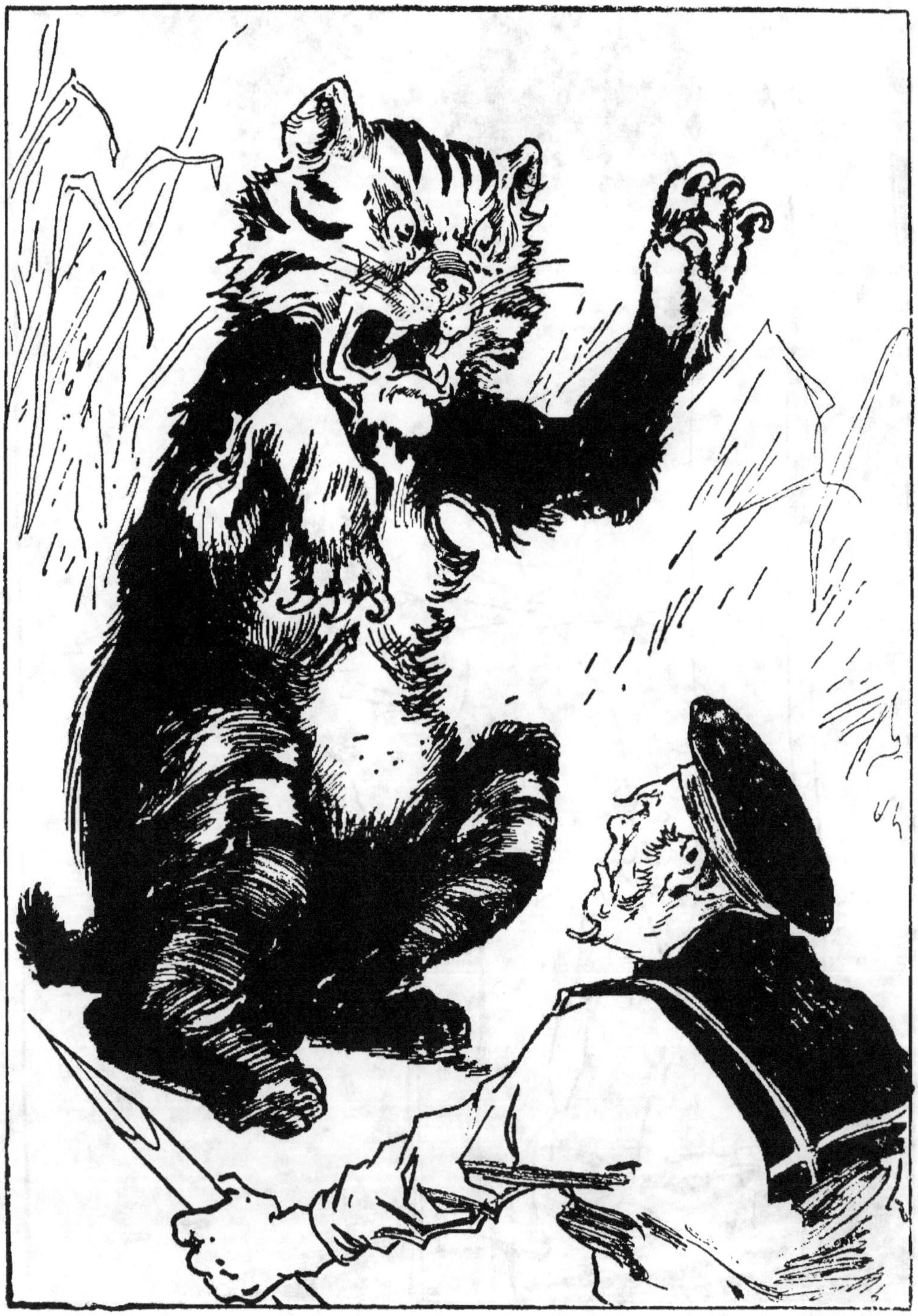

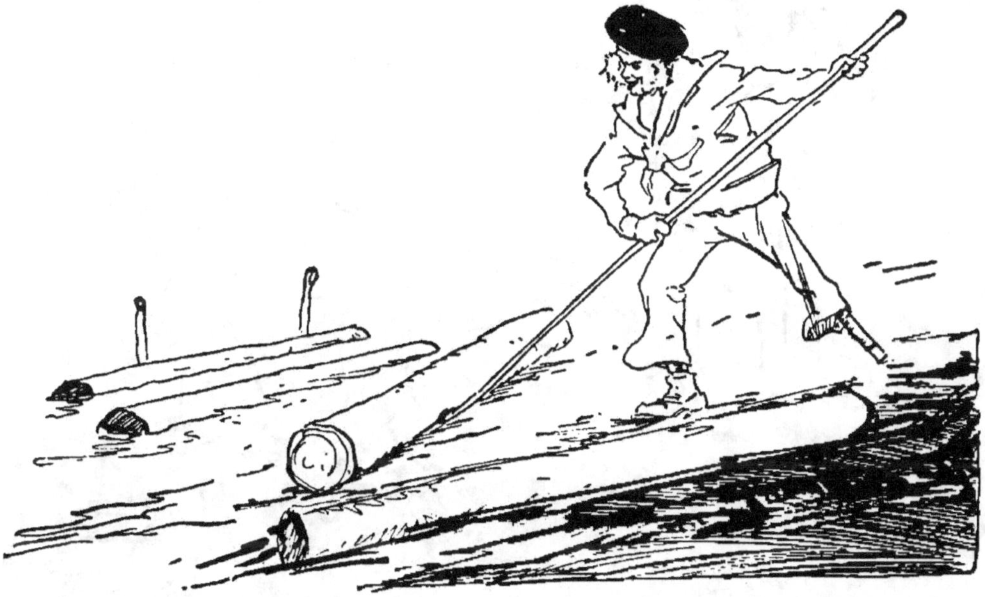

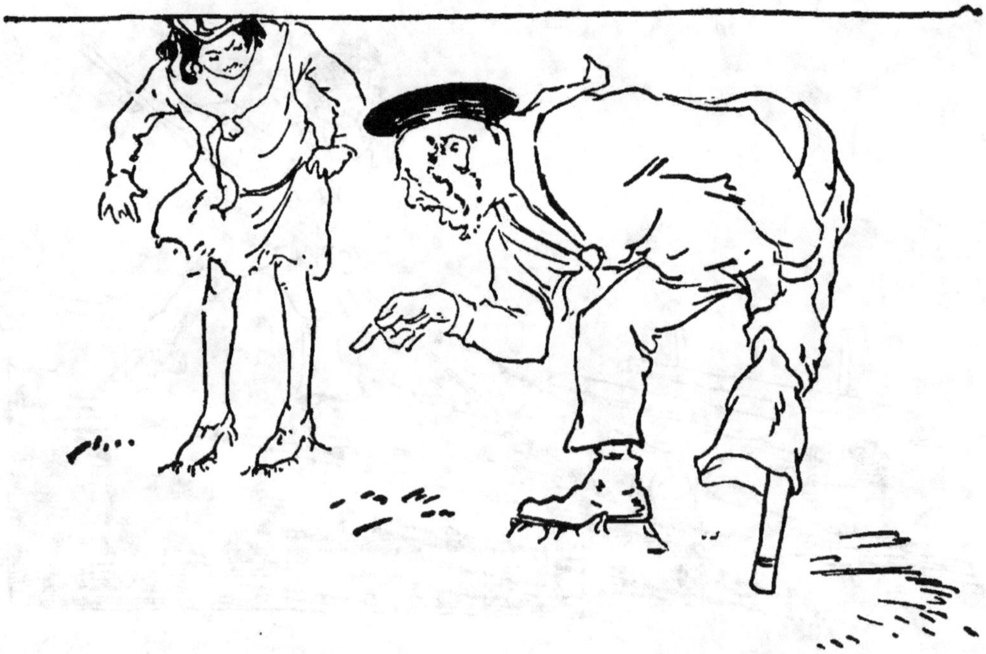

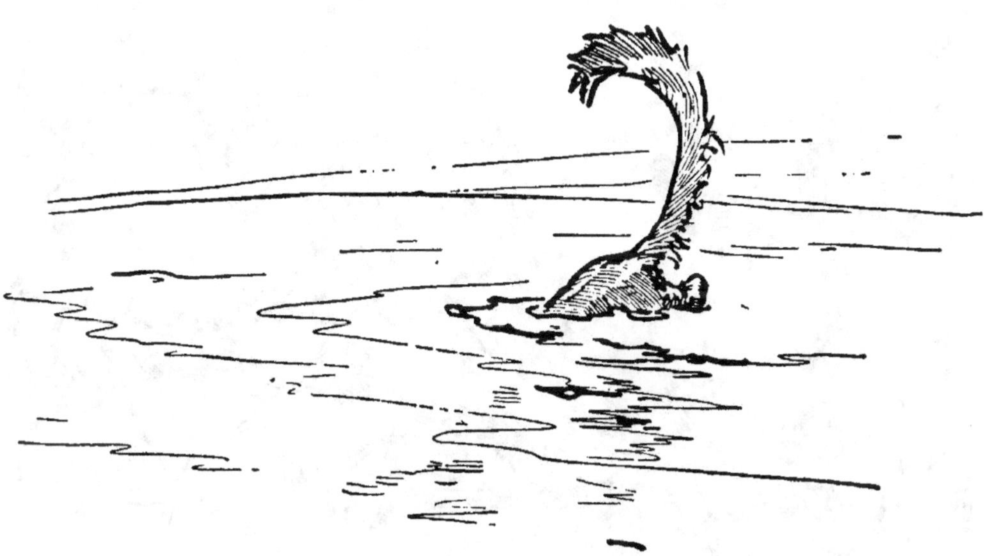

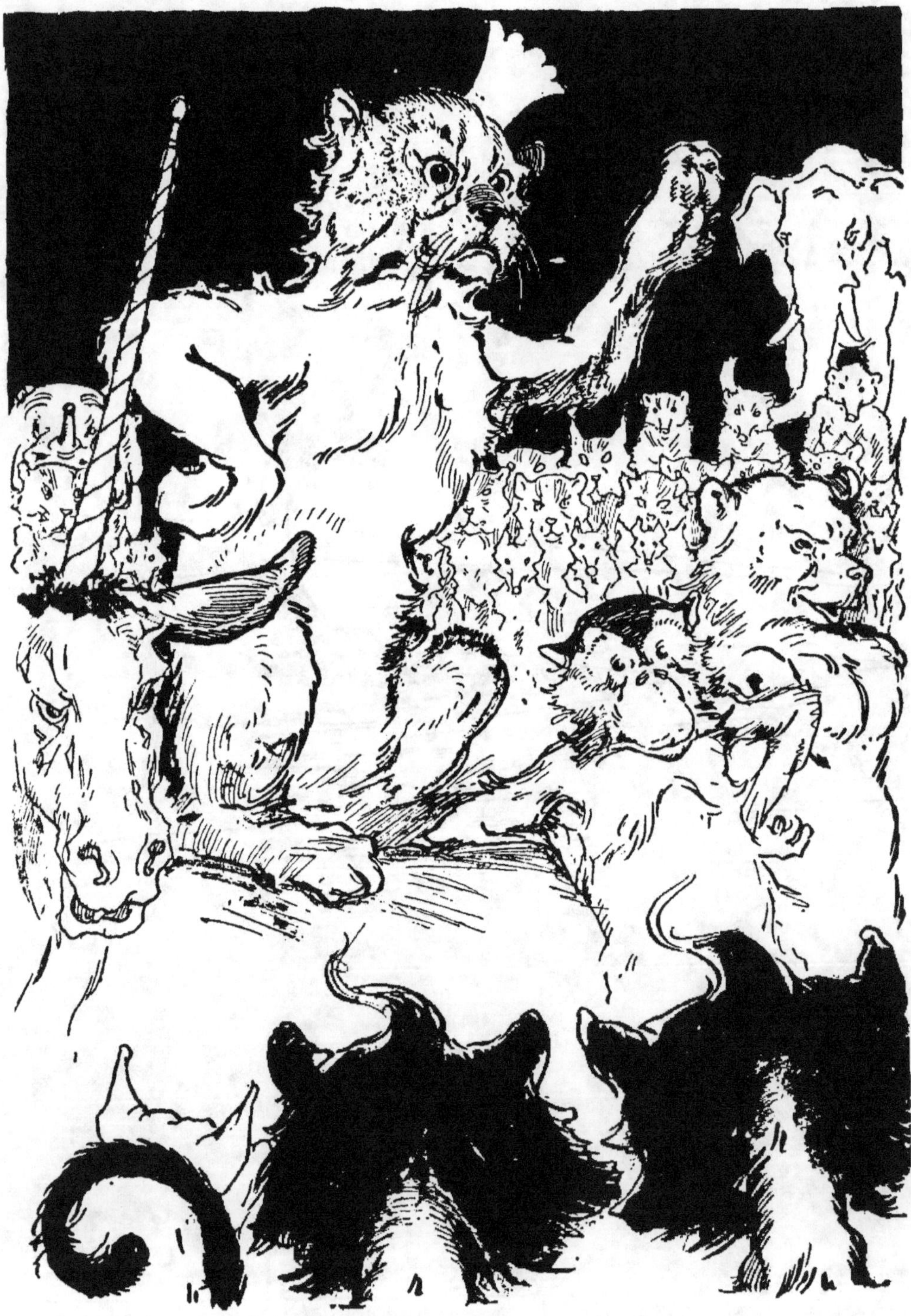

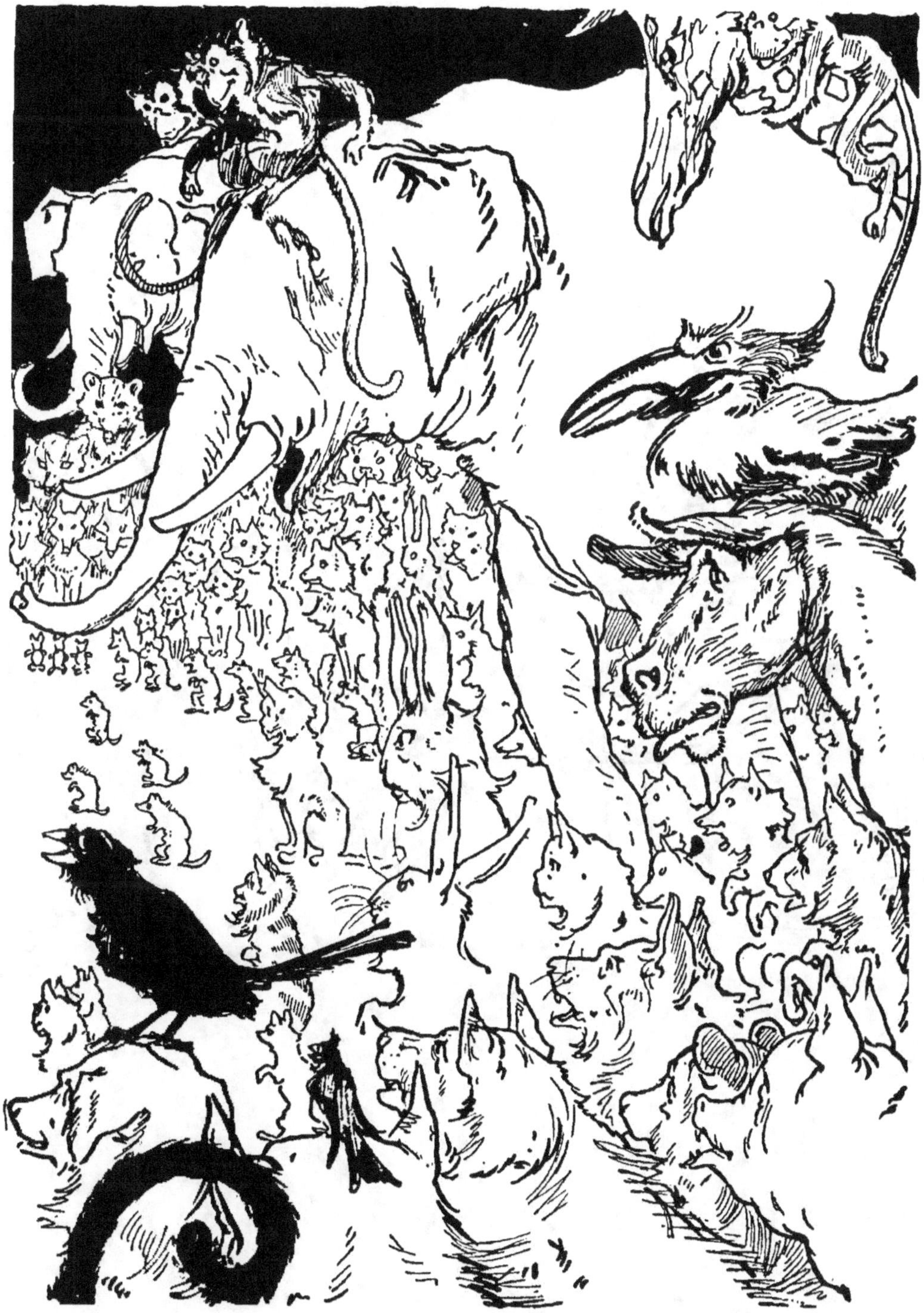

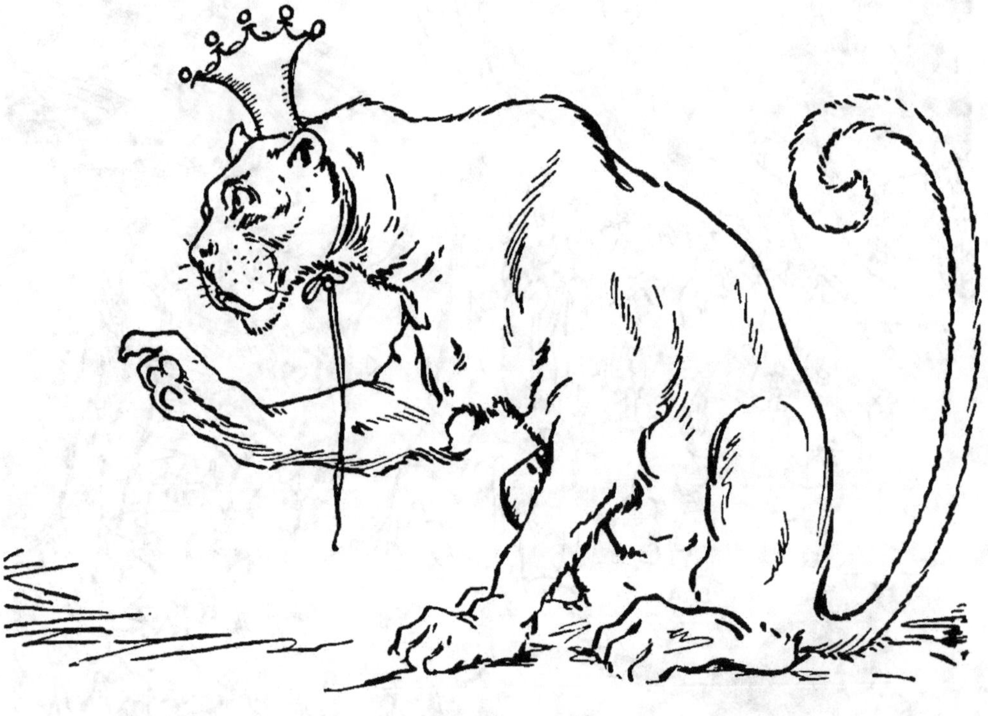

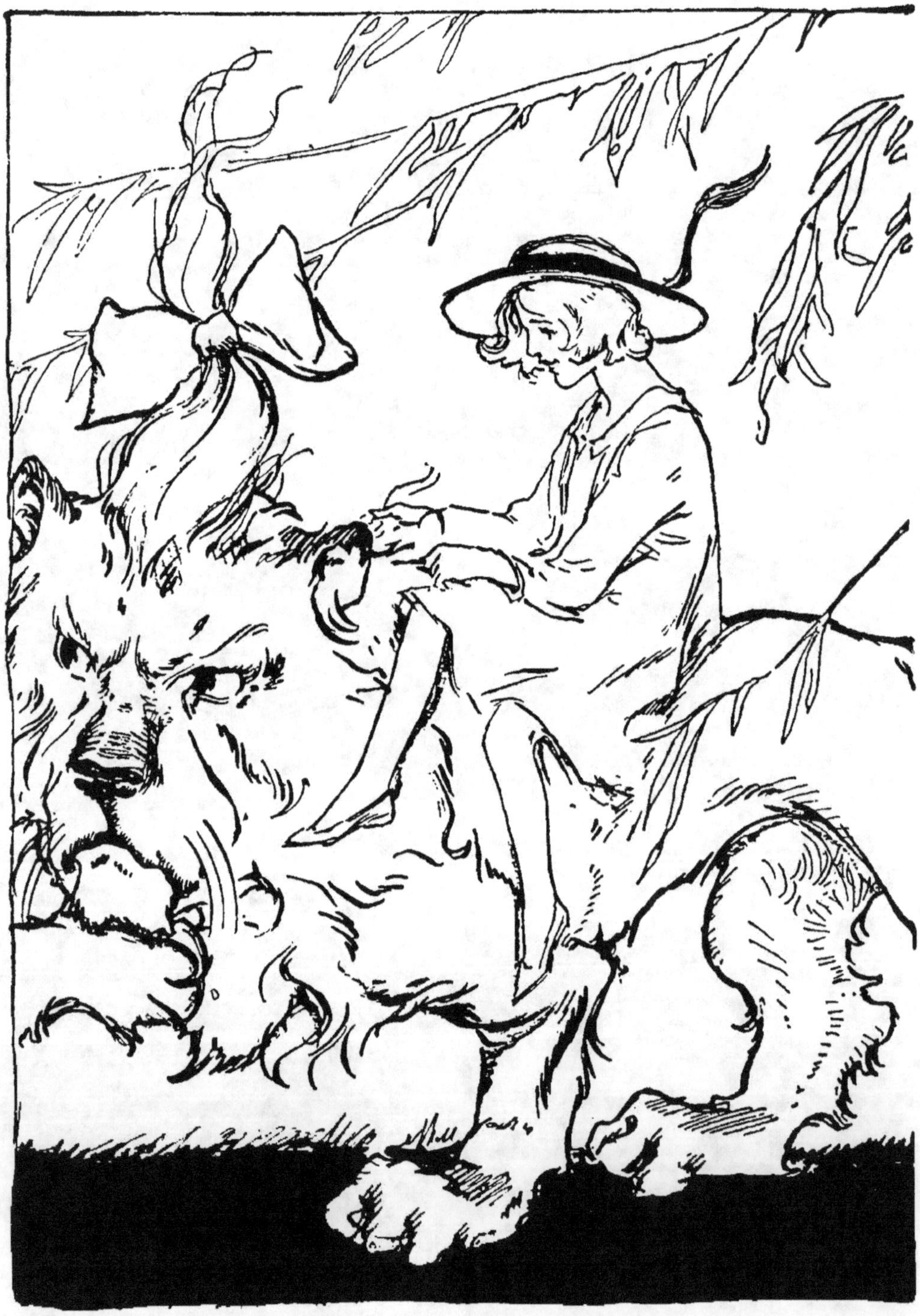

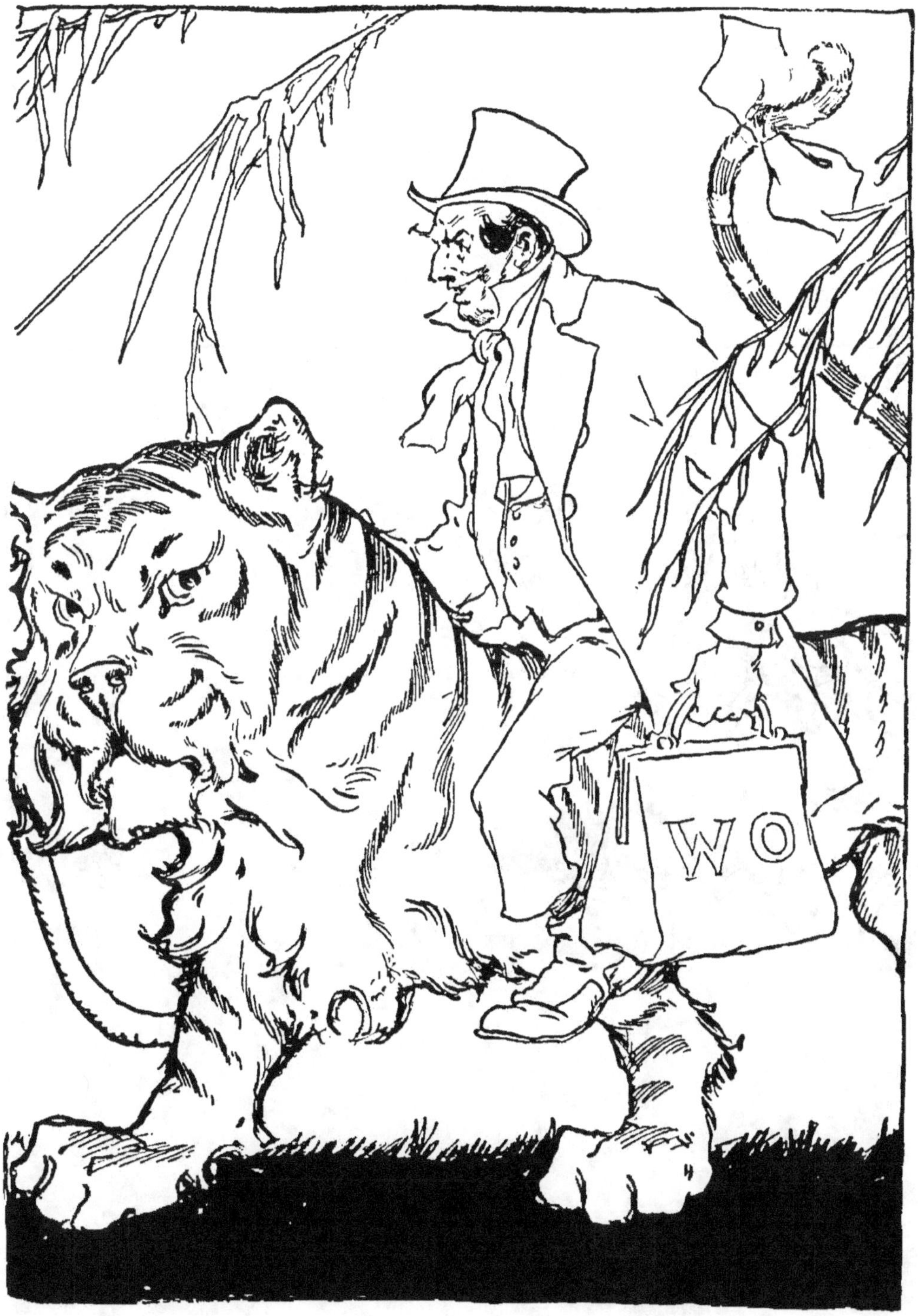
WO

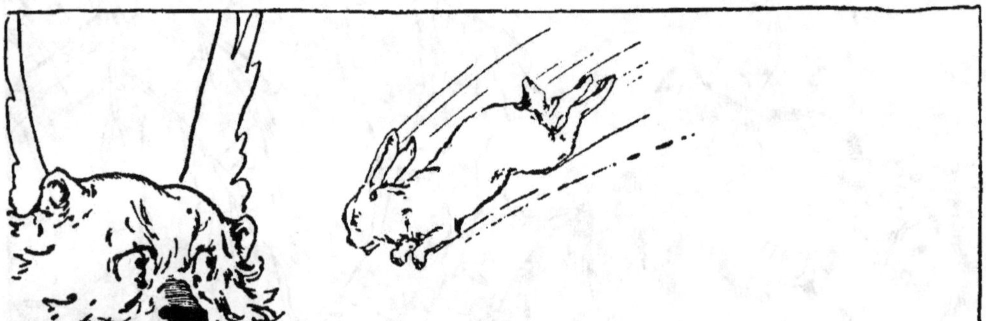

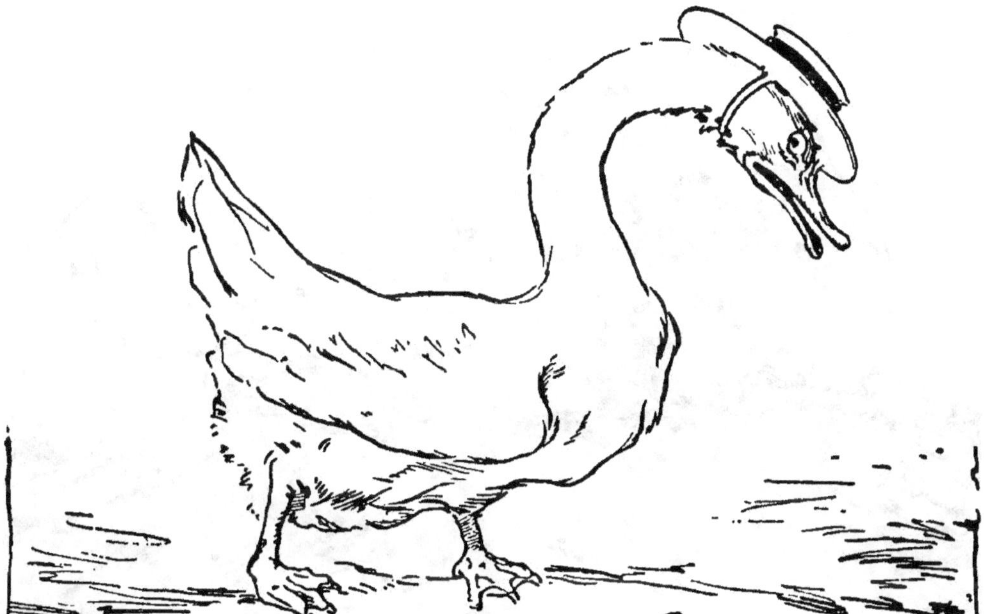

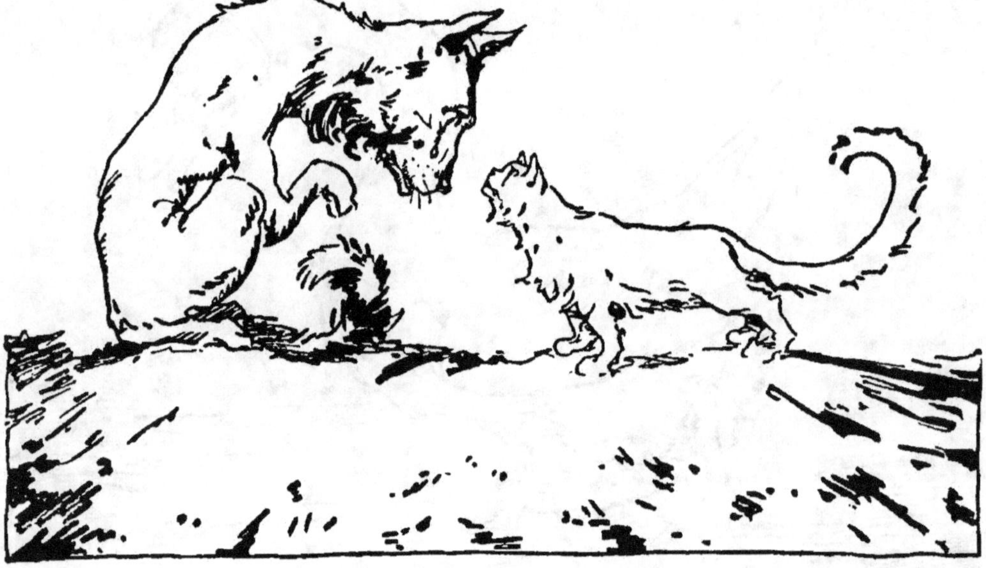

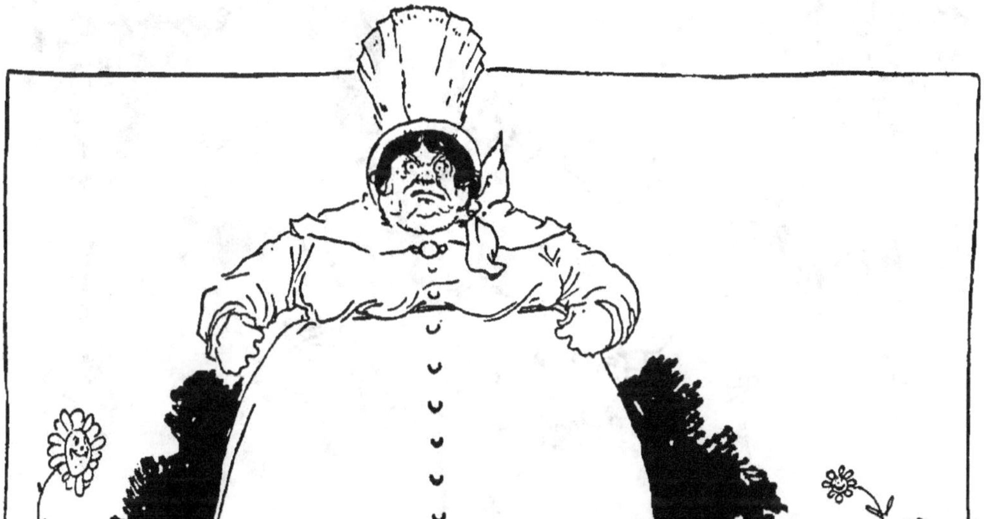

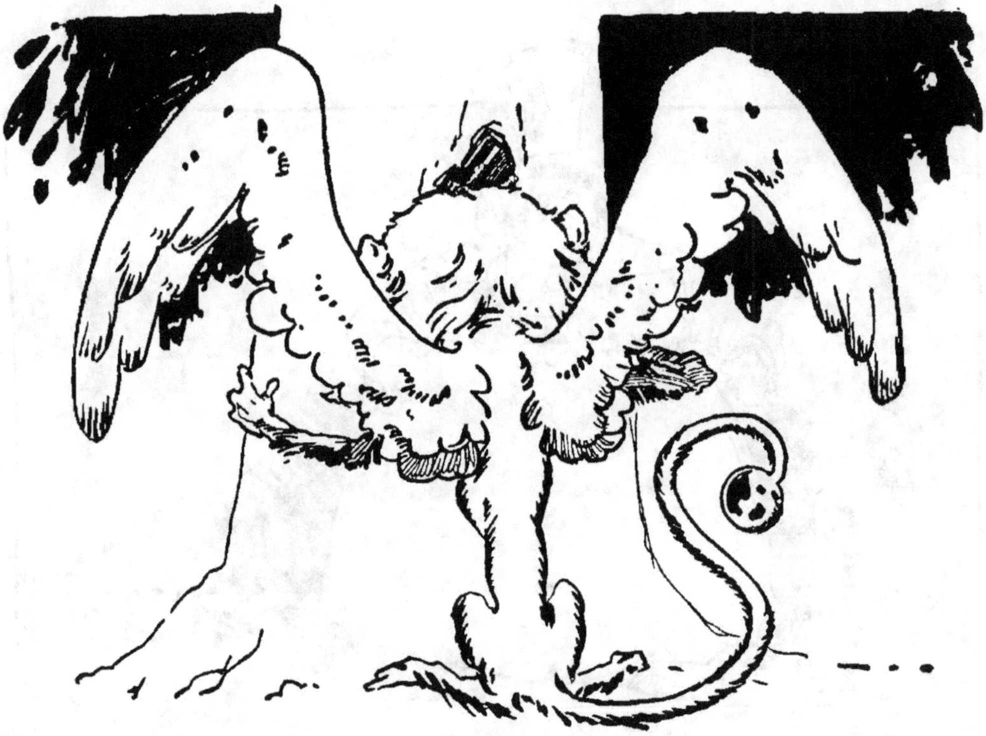

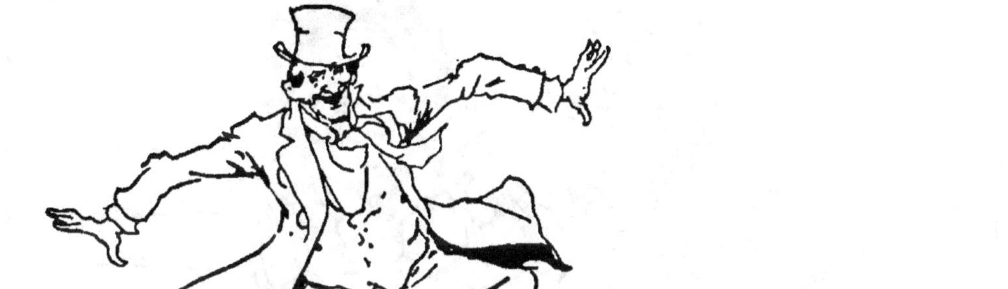

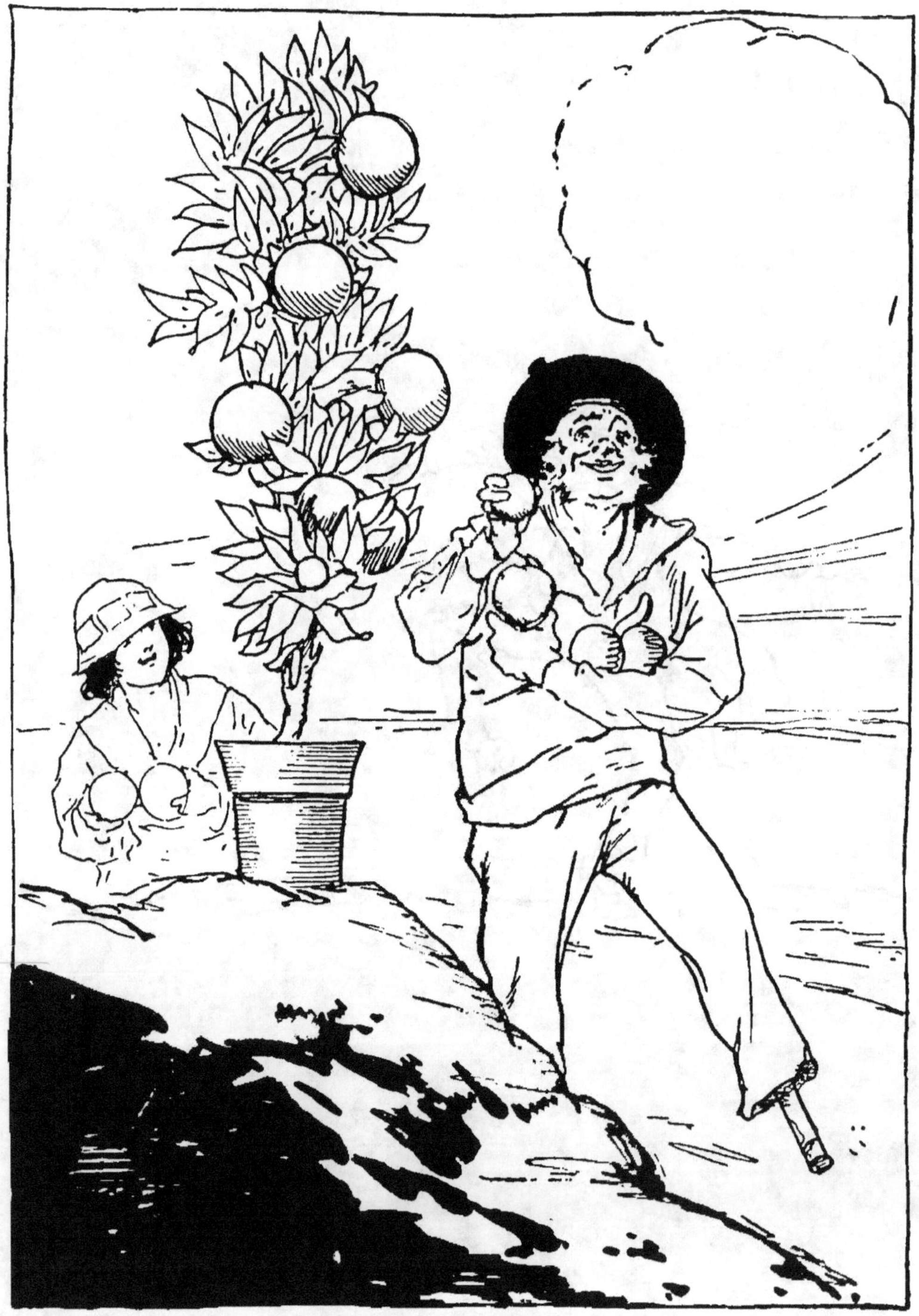

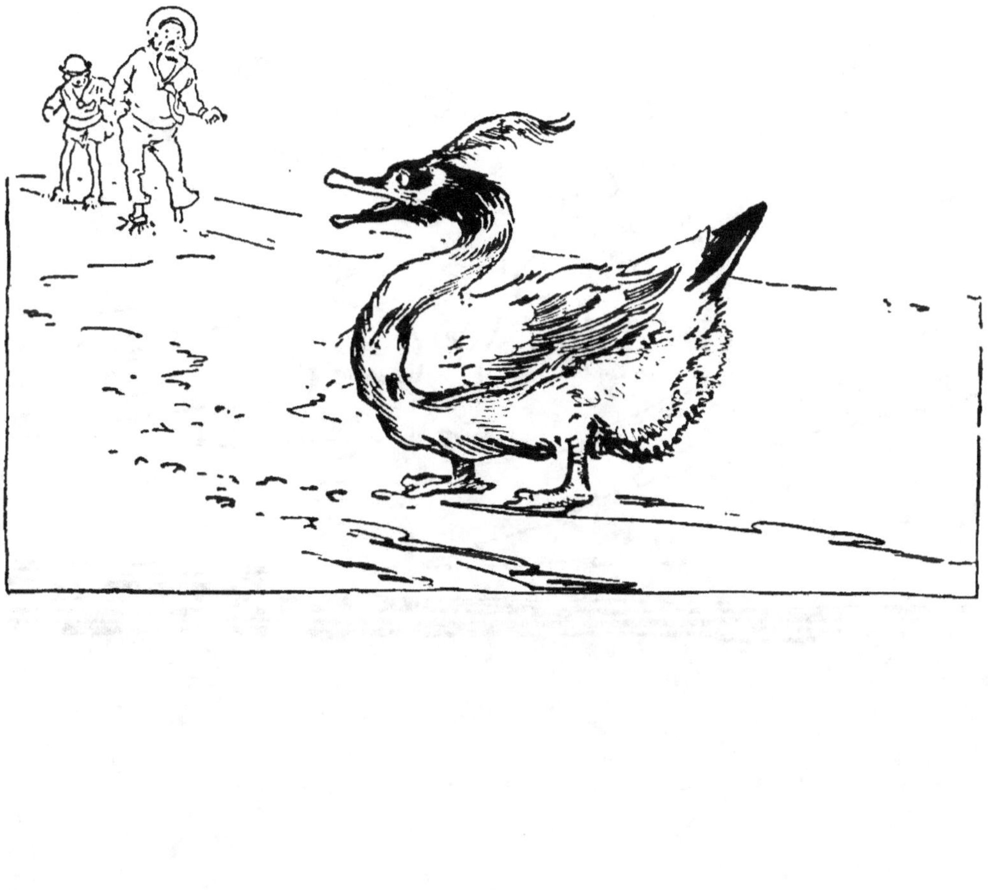

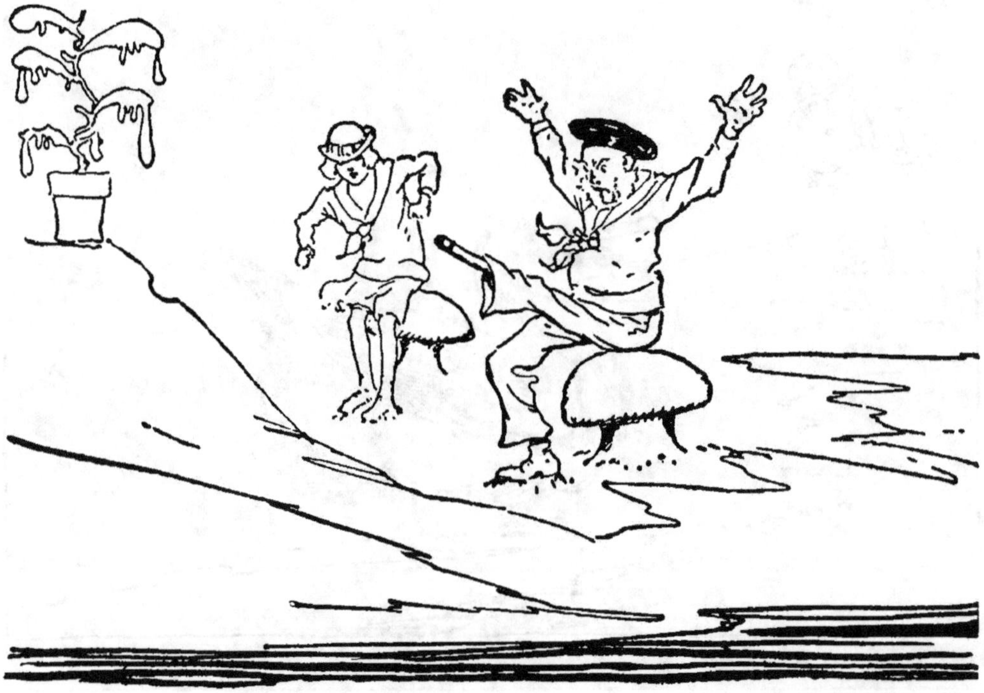

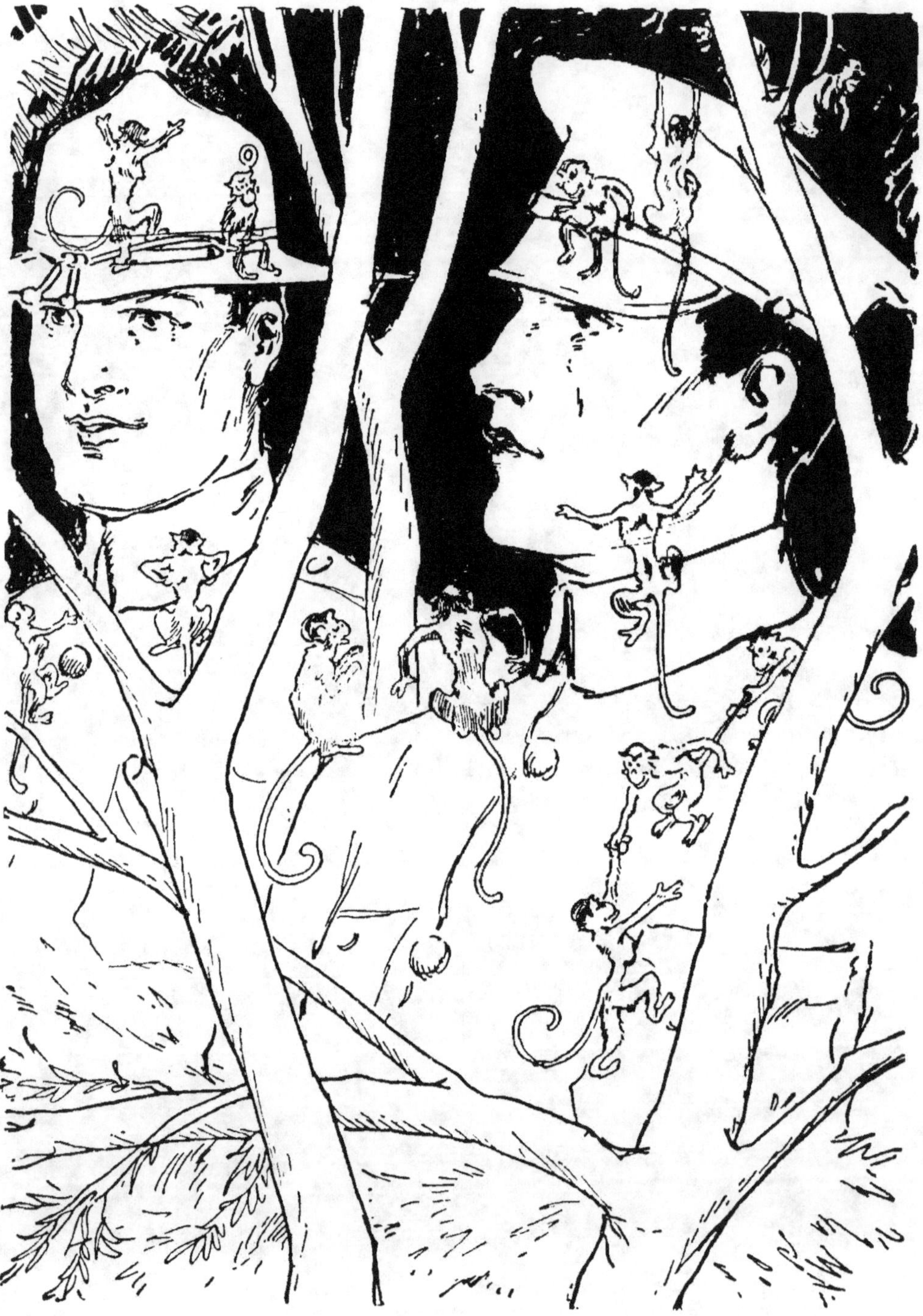

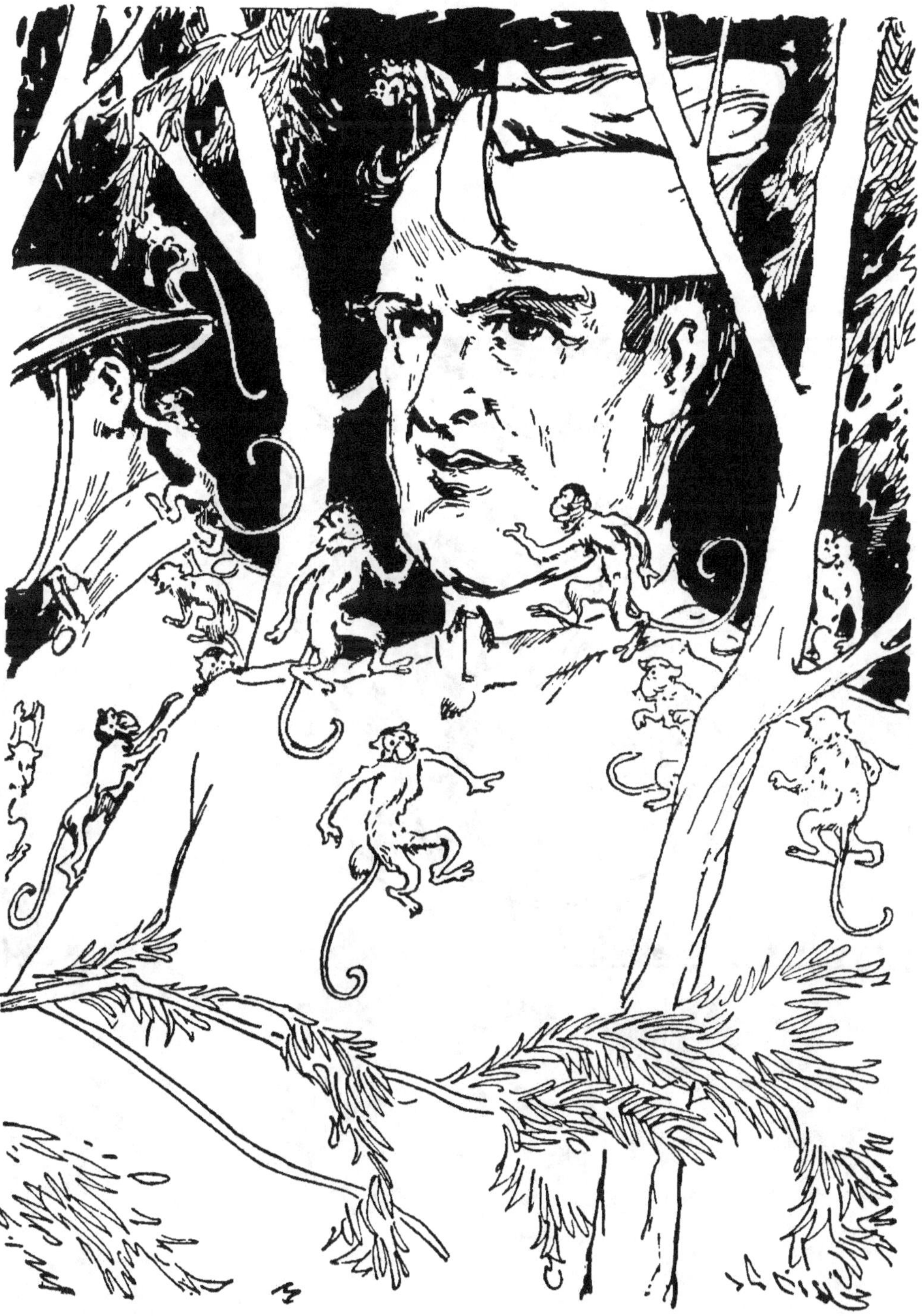

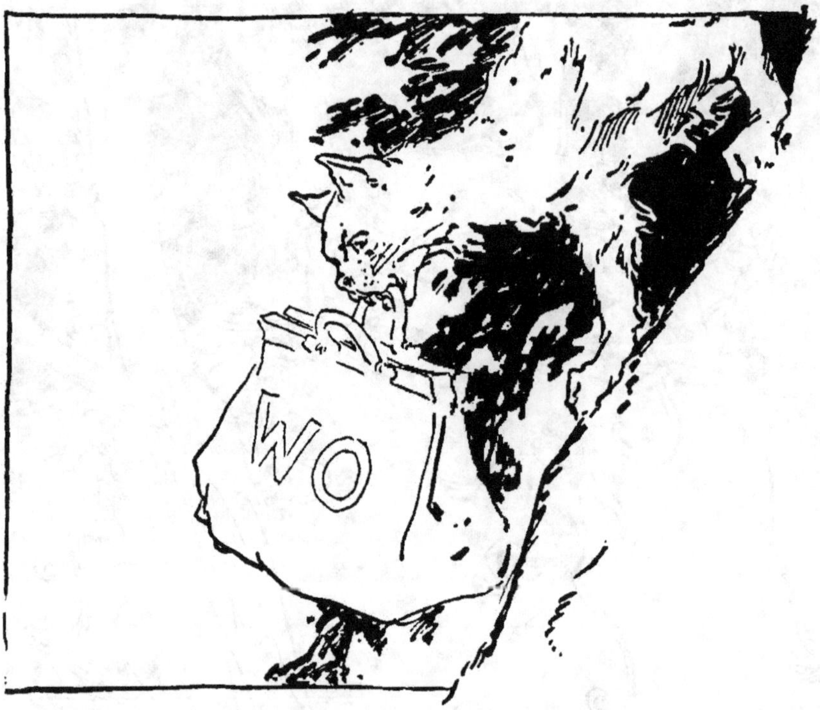
WO

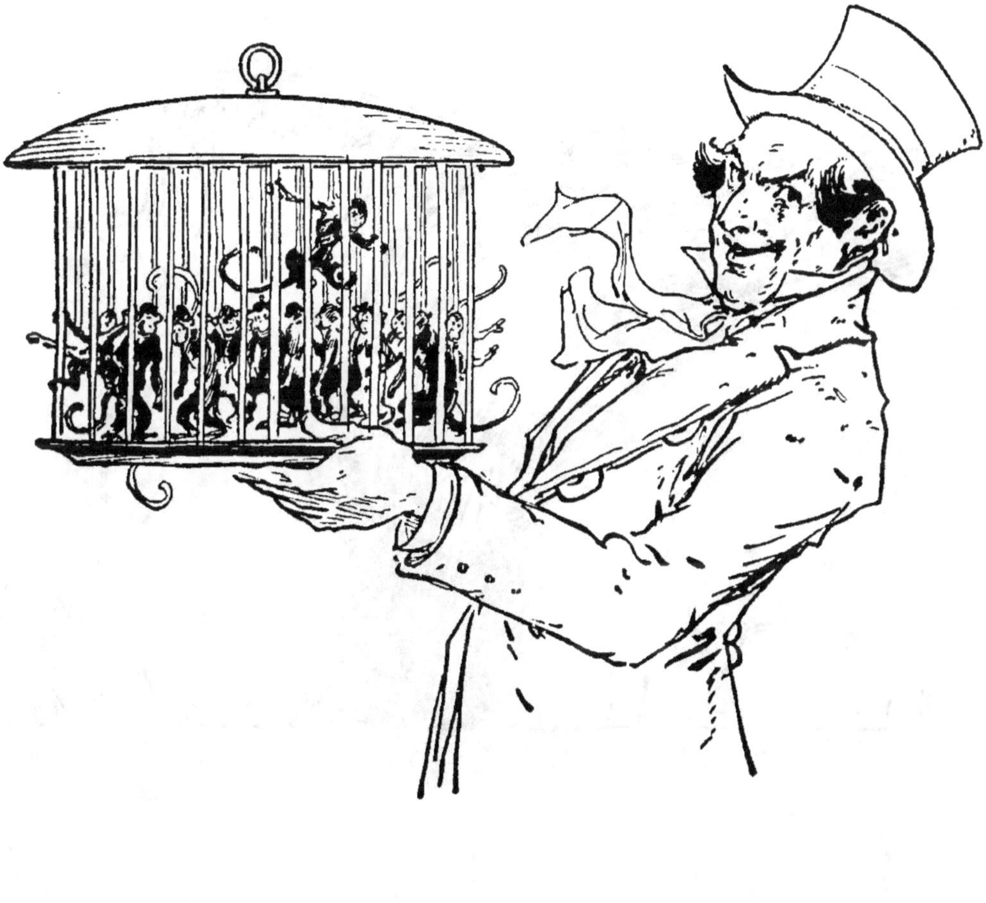

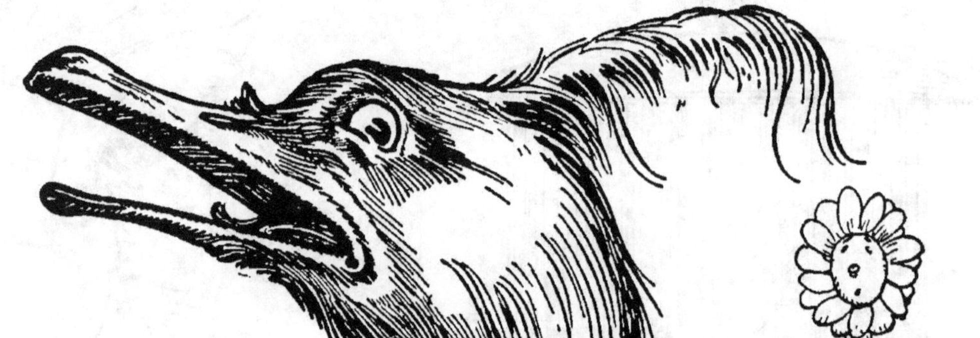

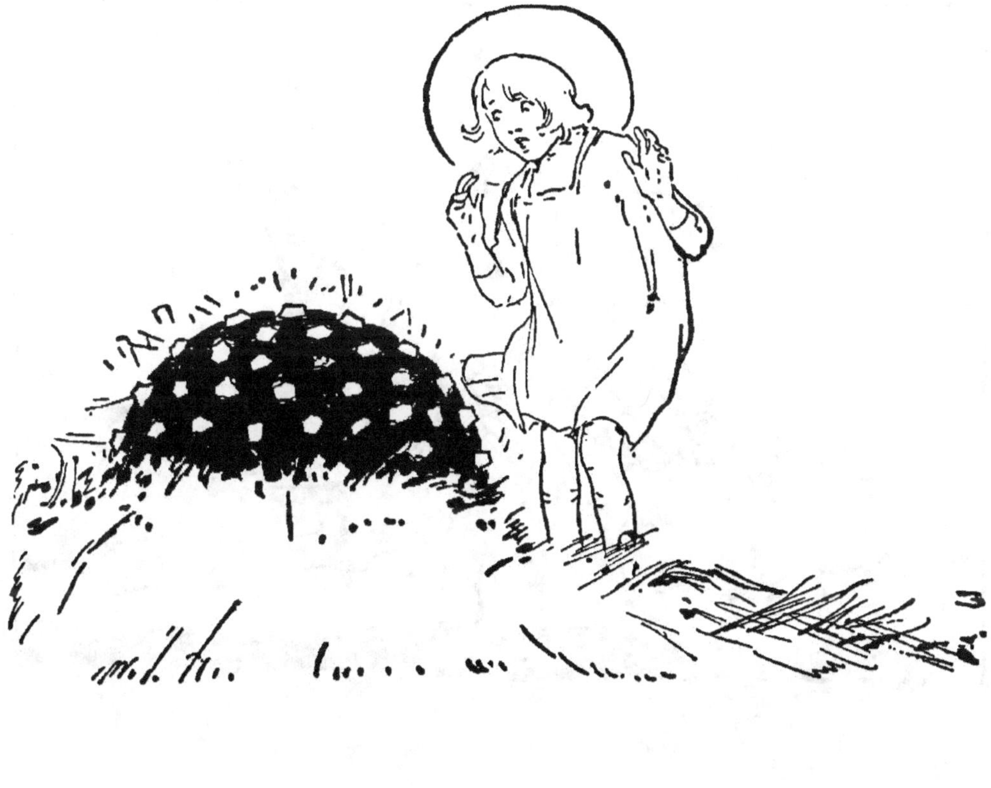

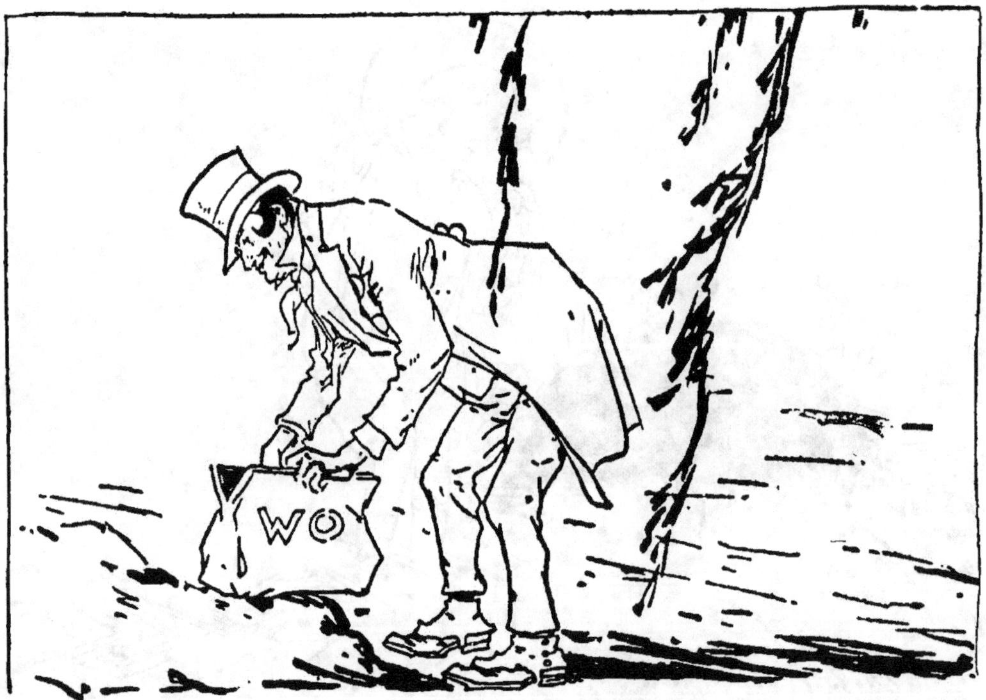
WO

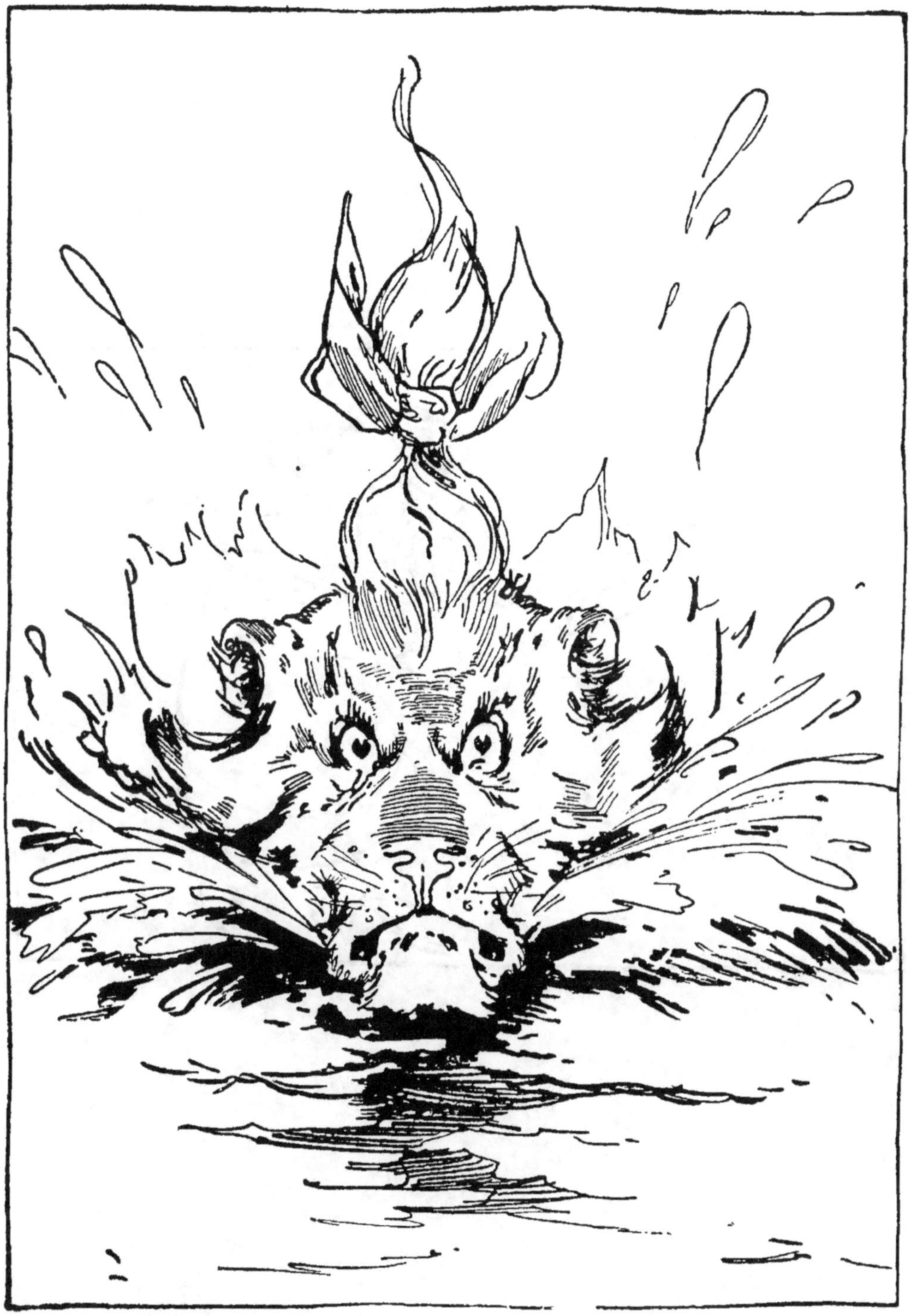

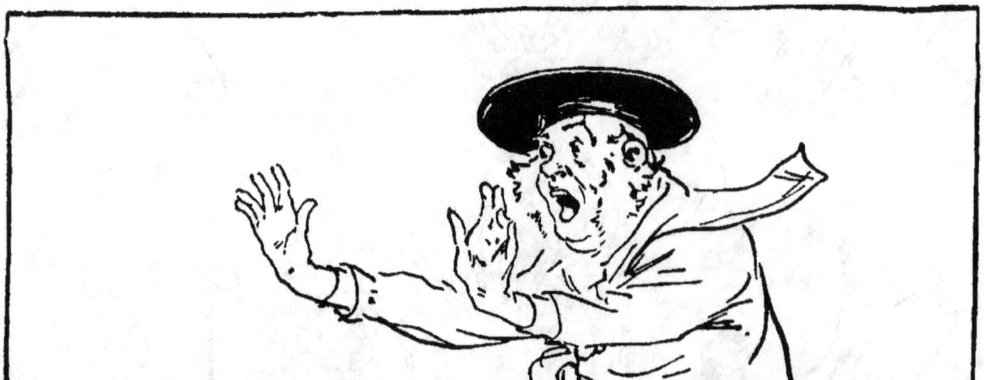

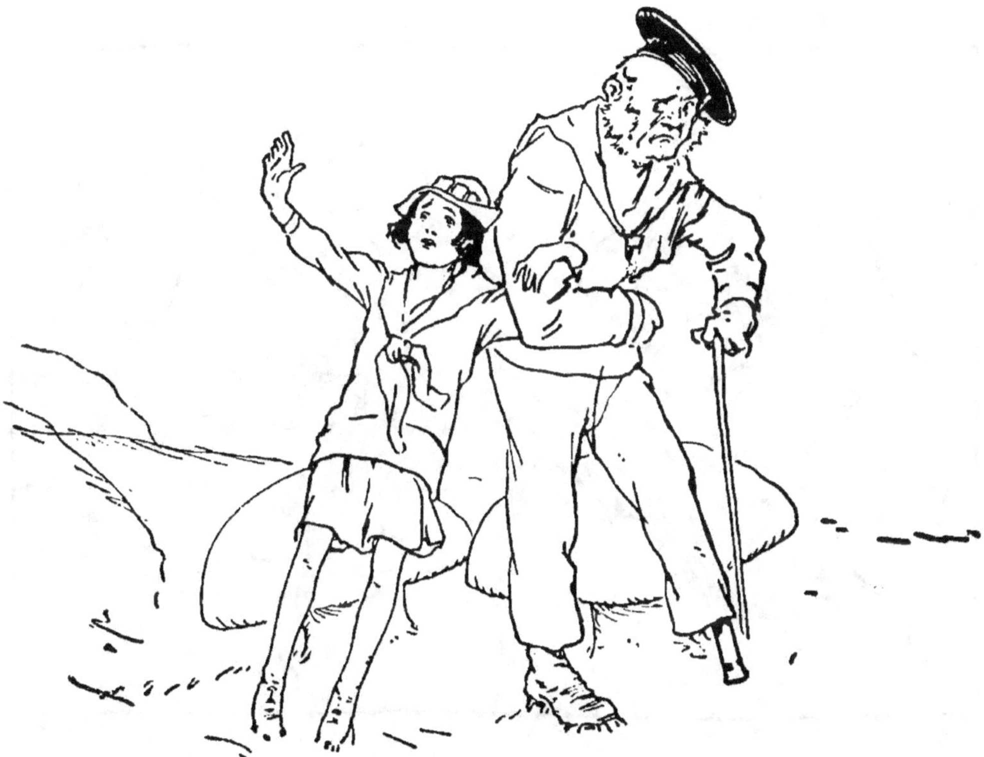

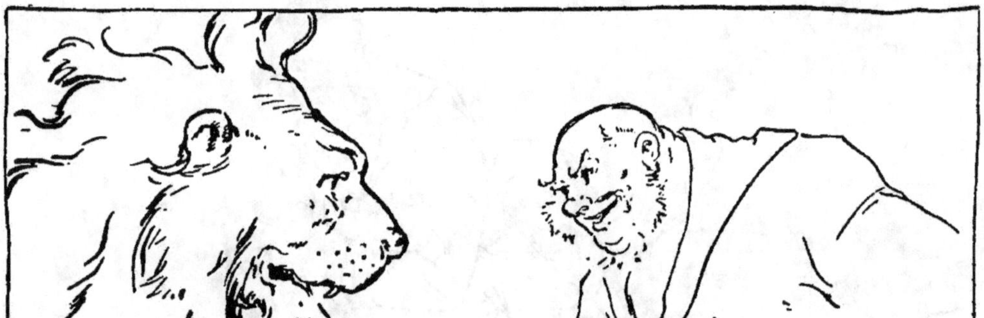

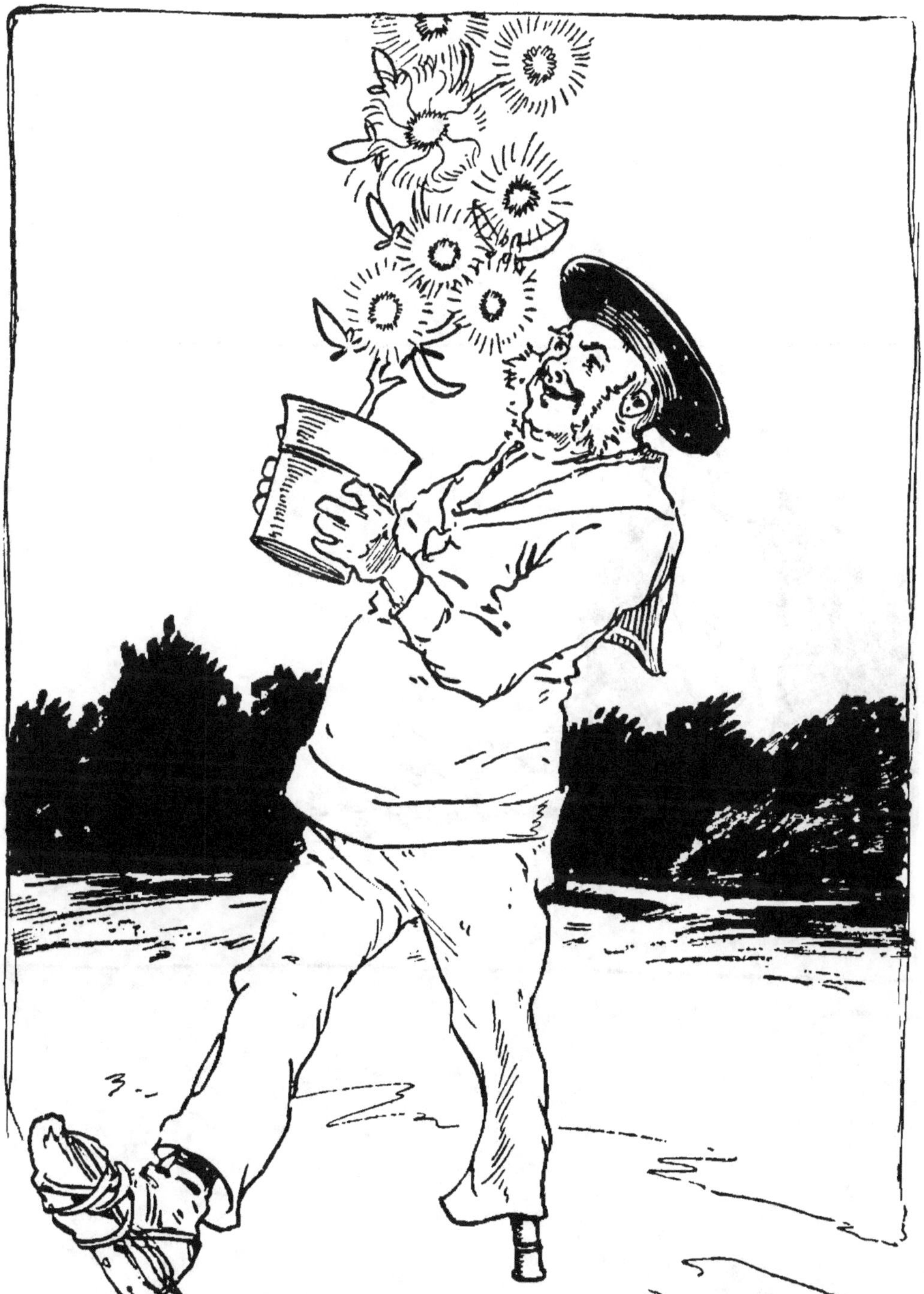

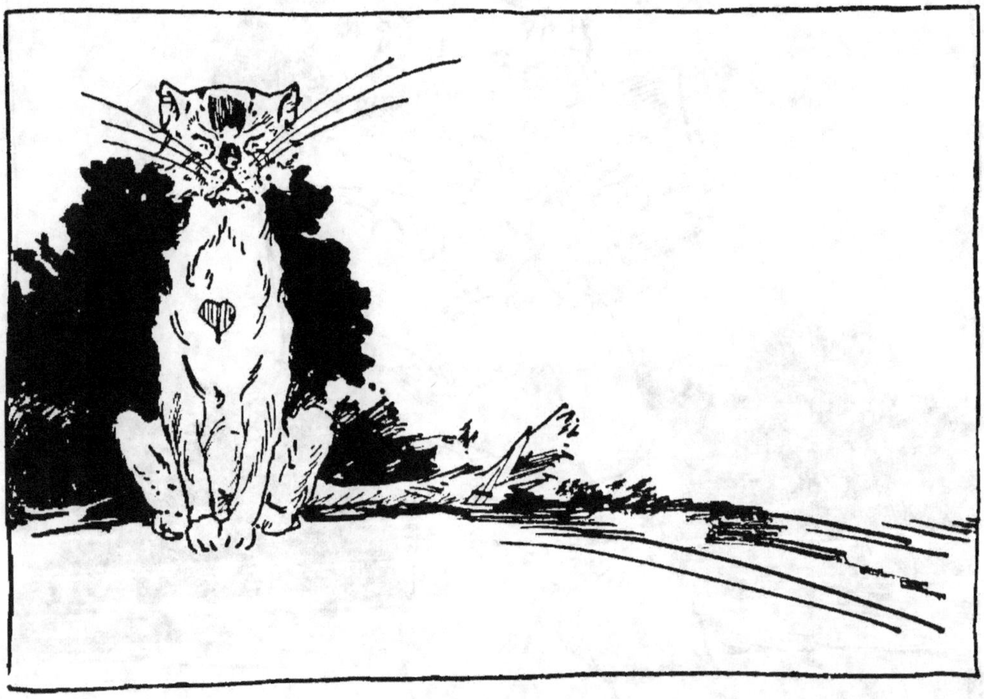

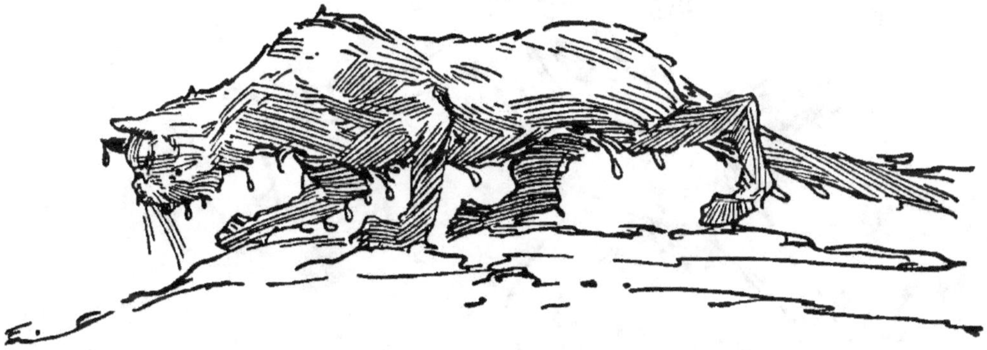

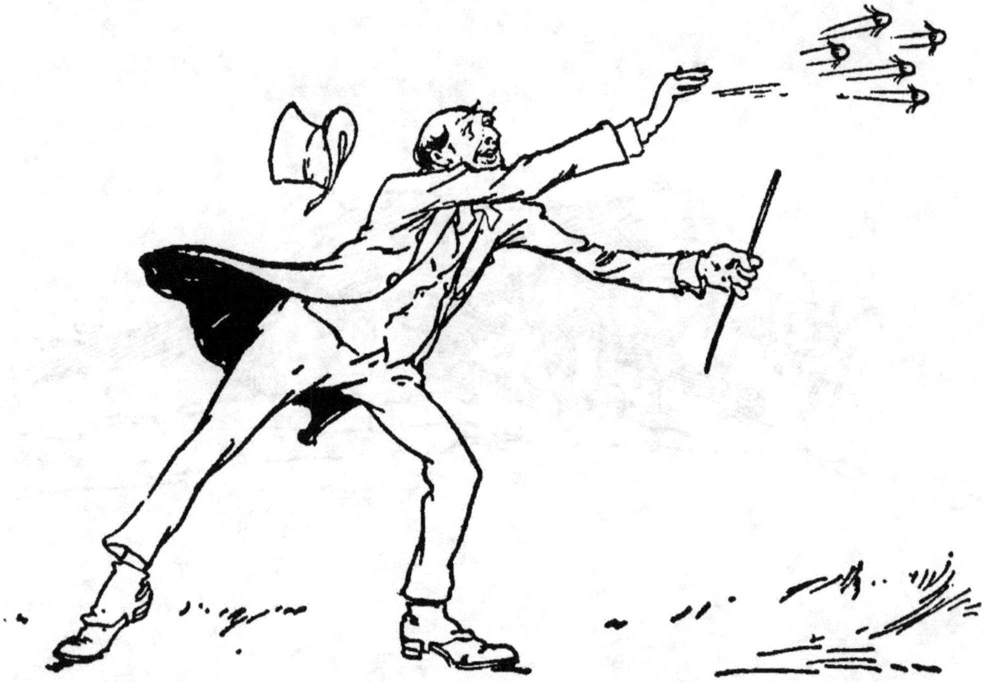

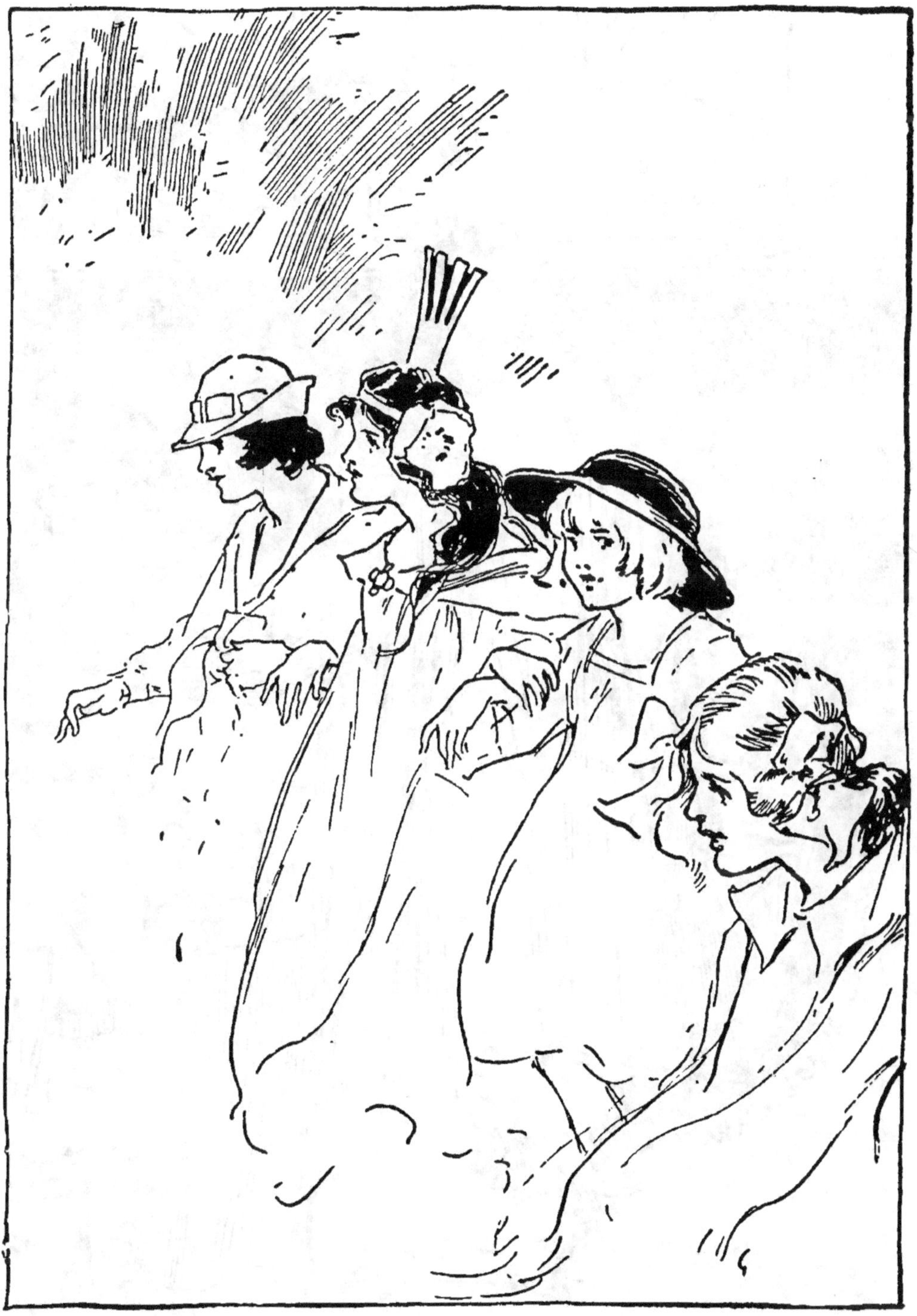

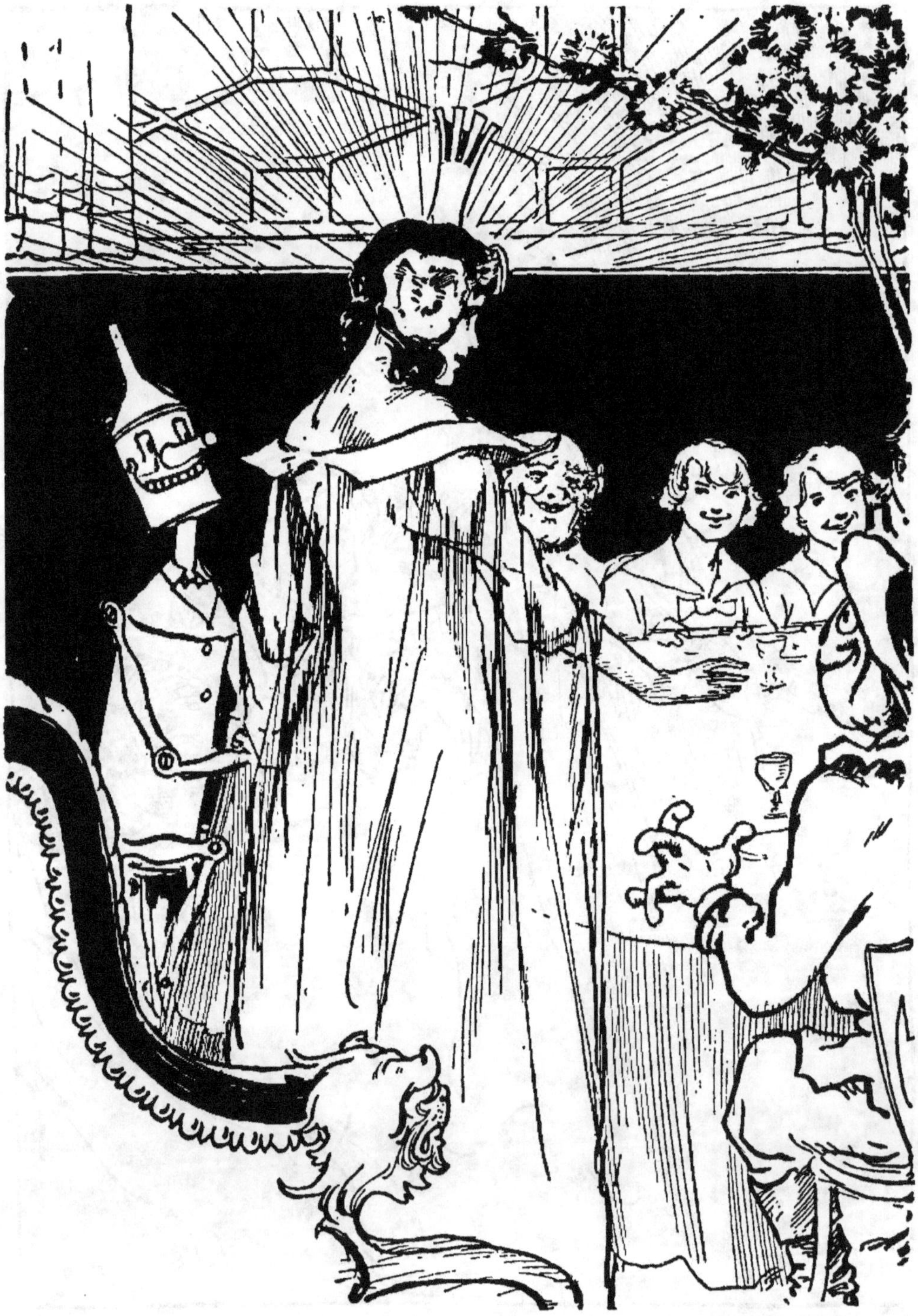

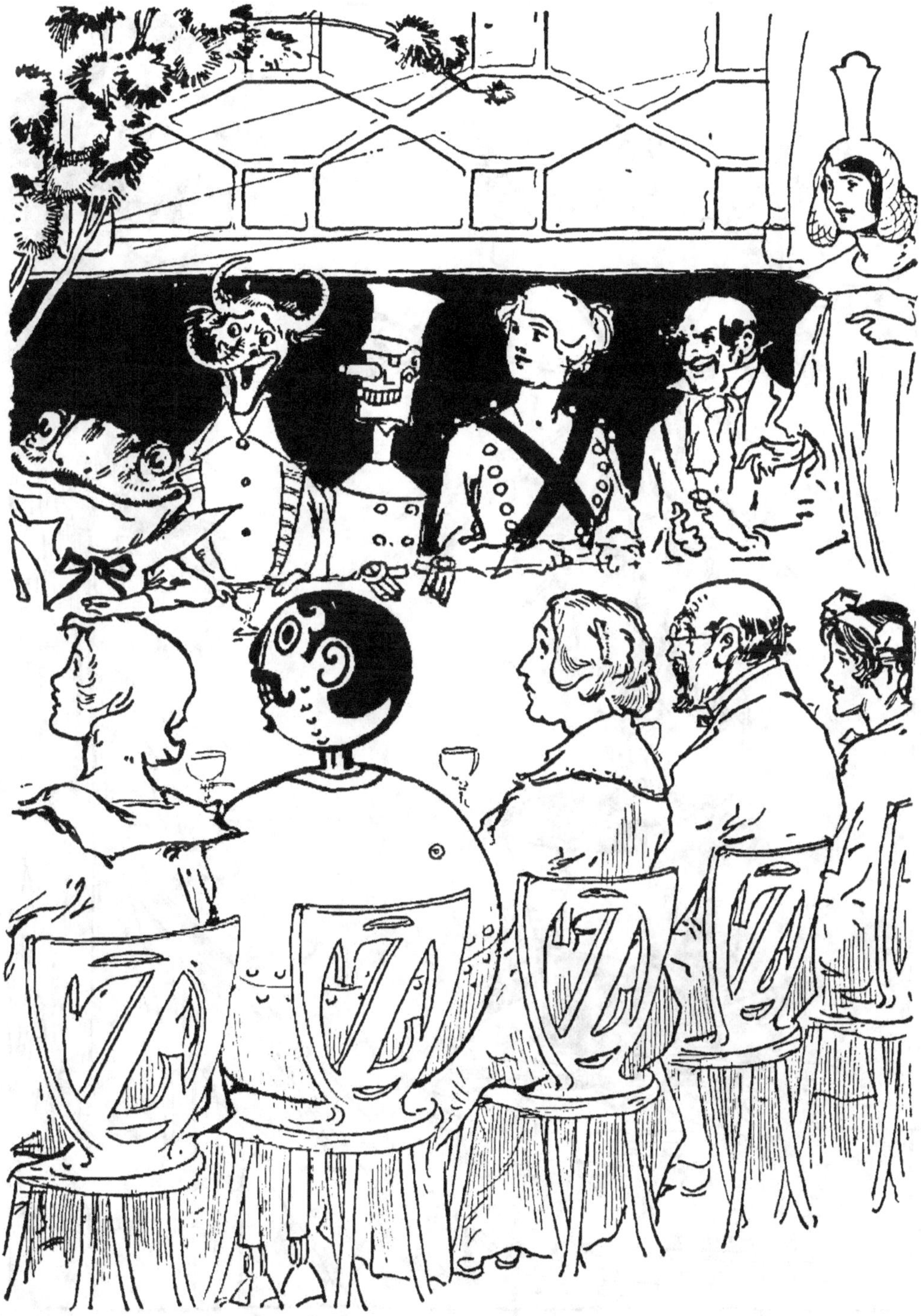

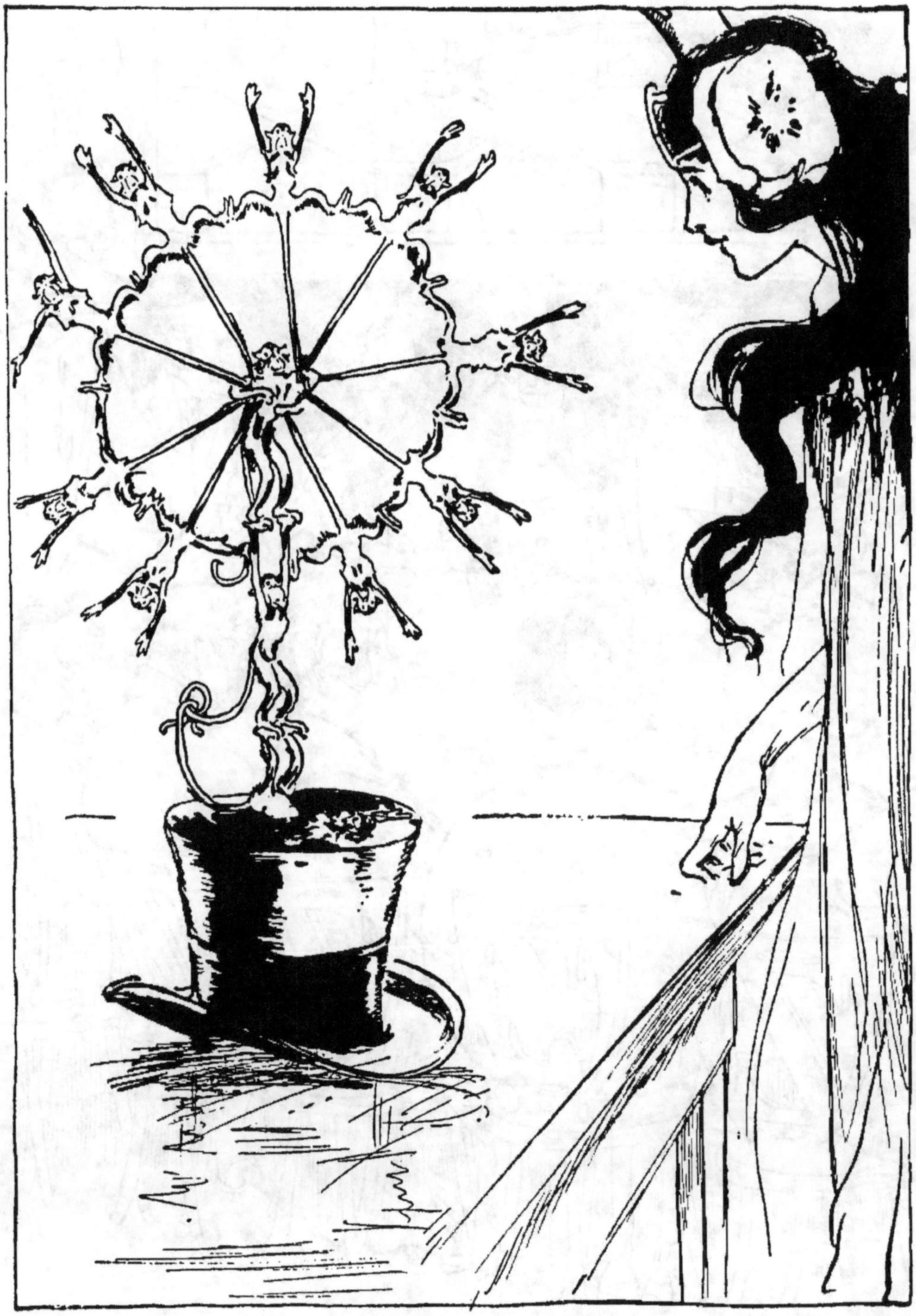

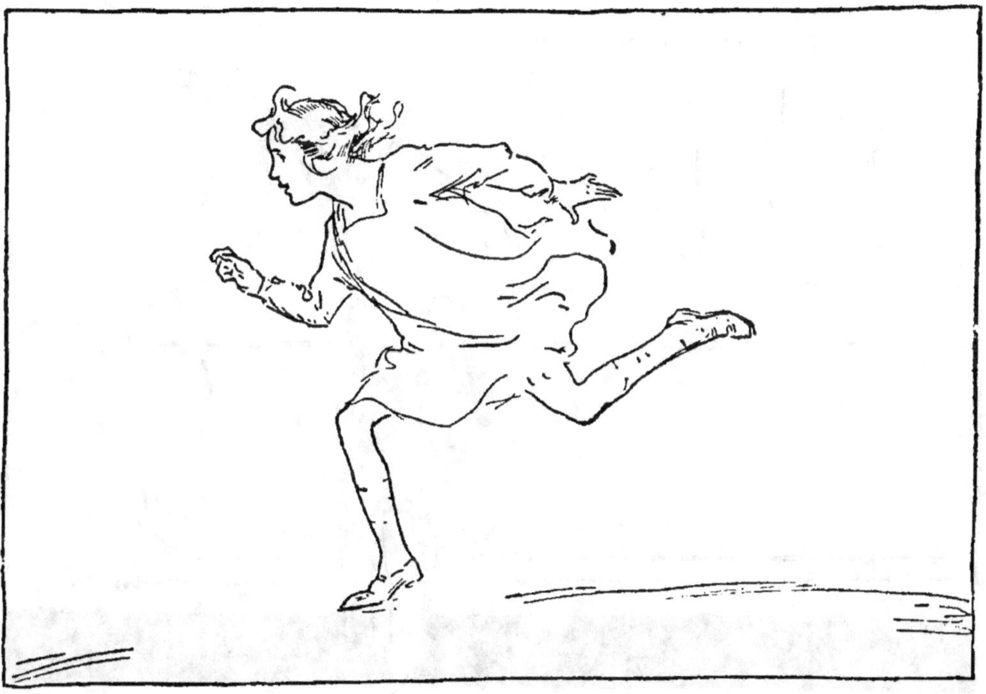

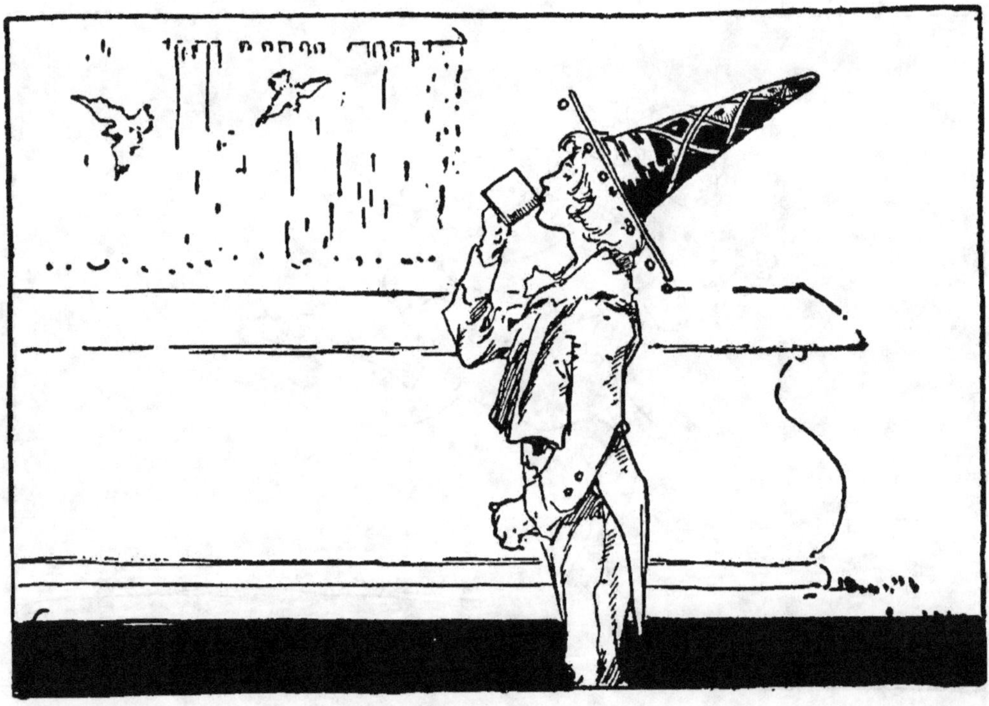

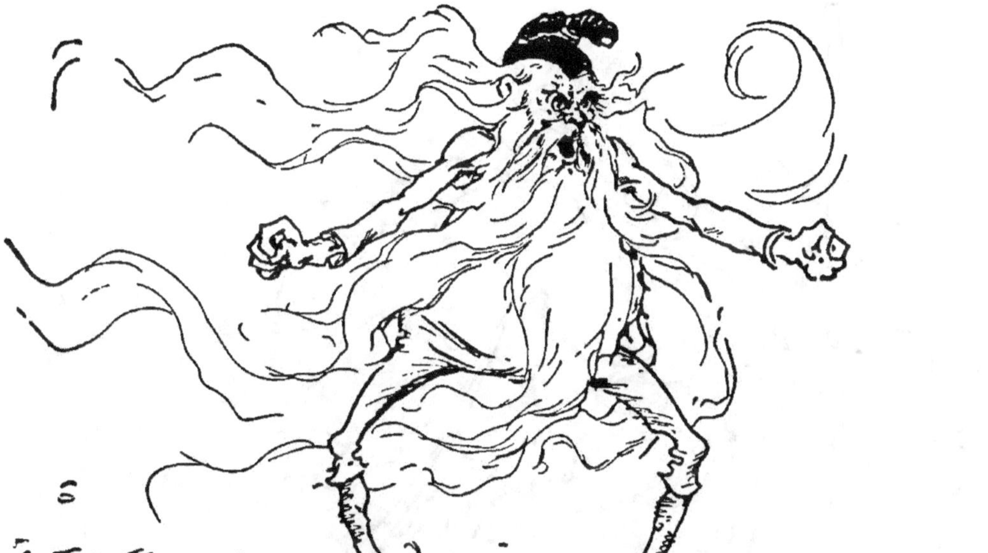

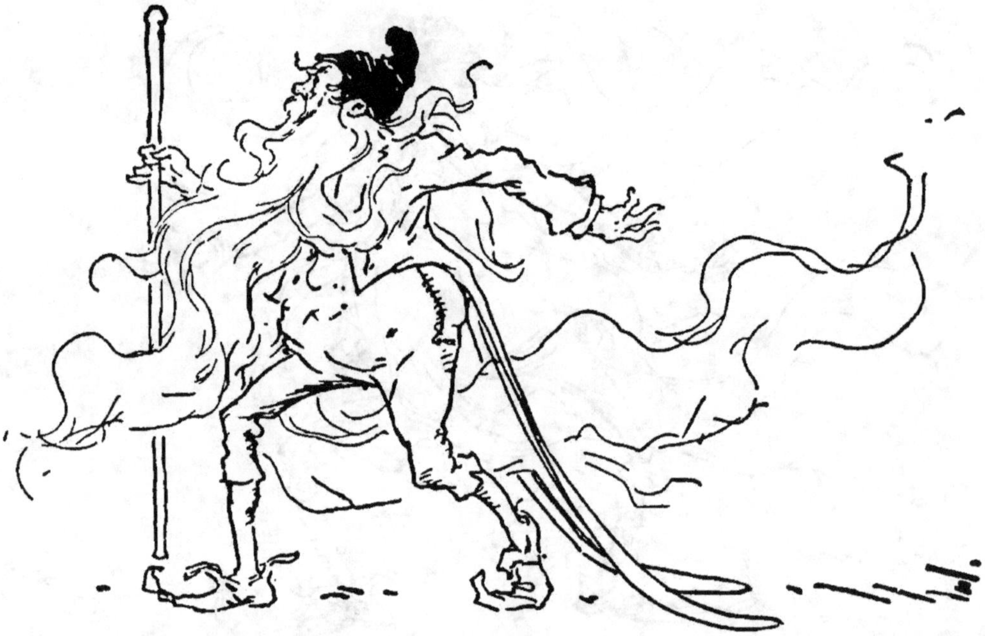

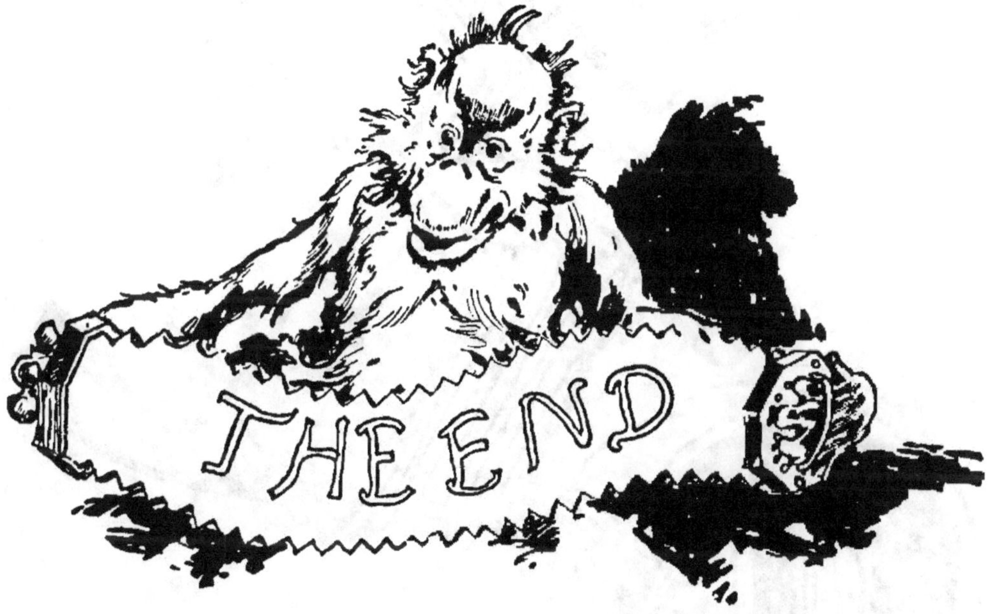
THE END

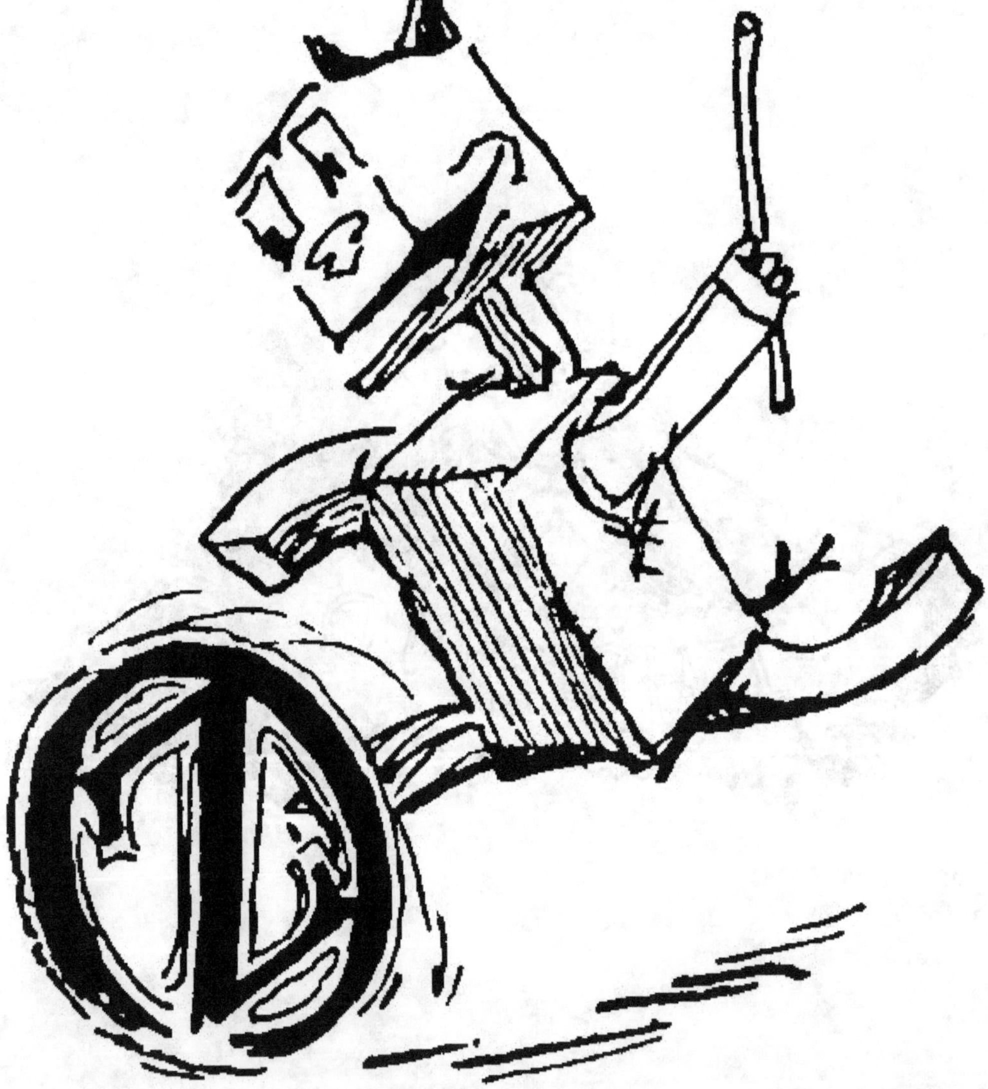

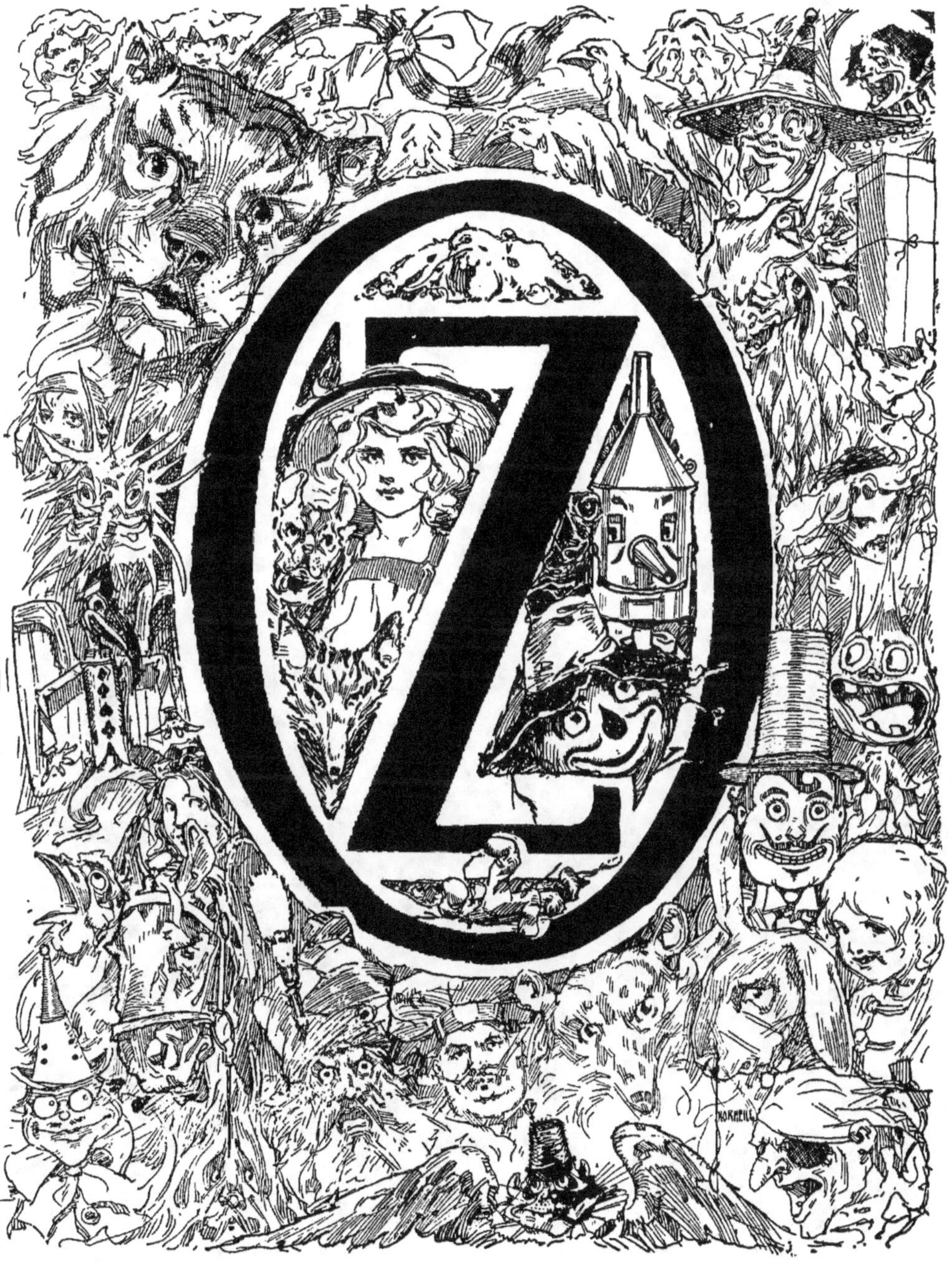
OZ

www.ingramcontent.com/pod-product-compliance
Lightning Source LLC
Chambersburg PA
CBHW081119180526
45170CB00008B/2921